Luom's Journey:
A Path of Past to Present View

By M D Fenton

PAGE PUBLISHING, INC.
New York, NY

First originally published by Page Publishing 2013

ISBN 978-1-62838-064-4 (pbk)
ISBN 978-1-62838-065-1 (digital)

Printed in the United States of America

This book is mainly for all my children: my daughters are Linda and Dawn; my sons are Casey, Arnold and Carl.

Also my grandchildren: Thao, Jenny, Emily, Hanna, Christopher, and all other in the future.

I'm proud of who I am and where I came from. I hope this book will be a treasure for my family after I'm gone.

Dear Ginny,

A year ago we were strangers. Without hesitation, I approached you and asked for you to help with my book. You happily accepted. Your patience and your good heart have taught me new things. Thank you for your support me and I appreciate all the time you have given me. I treasure our friendship.

Love

M D Fenton

Dear Aline,

Thank you for your help with my book. Because of this book, I feel that our relationship has grown exponentially. Through you I have learned many things. One is how to be your Auntie. Thank you for your support and your patience.

Love your Auntie

M D fenton

Prologue

Heavy rain fell down all night. Lightning flashes crossed the sky, flooded through the window, and Thunder Angel shook up the heaven with his roars. It woke Luom. Her eyes glued on the alarm clock: 1:00 AM. Luom tried to go back to sleep, but it was impossible. Not wanting to disturb her husband on a Saturday morning with her tossing and turning, Luom softly got out of the bed. Quietly, she moved in the dark across the floorboards and headed down to the kitchen.

Through patio glass, lights from the hill of Spring Valley twinkled, looking like the lights of the Christmas season. Down in the back of her house, Sunny Side Valley farmhouses lay still in darkness. She could hear the rooster's uniquely crowing call. The open field below reminded her of Viet Nam, her homeland. Beyond the valley, Spring Valley Lake was also shrouded, yet when daytime came, the scene from her kitchen window would be worth a million glances. Luom's husband, Chris, pleased his wife with a house amidst a stunning countryside, fulfilling one of her dreams.

Rain had poured down for days, with gusty weather. The palm trees in her backyard bent in the wind, like the pinnate of the coconut trees in Viet Nam, swinging backward and forward in monsoon season. Luom's mind gently traveled back into her past.

At nights before bedtime, Luom's family gathers on the divan around a little oil lamp under the roof of coconut foliage. Luom's father, Mr. Bay, is a family storyteller. Mrs. Danh, Luom's mother, carries in a little pot of Jasmine tea surrounded by four miniature cups. She places the tray with a tobacco water pipe in the center of the divan. Putting the pipe into his mouth, Mr. Bay inhales the smoke from his pipe and exhales with a cough. The family members are always a good audience. To make sure everyone will stay and listen, Mrs. Danh usually prepares some chicken soup.

Mrs. Danh asks her parents in-law, "Father and Mother, should I serve you my chicken soup?"

Mr. Ngoc answers his daughter in-law, "Yes daughter, I would like to have some of your chicken soup."

Mrs. Ho Thiet also agrees with her husband, "Yes daughter, I'll have some too."

Mrs. Danh turns to her husband and asks, "Minh Oi (honey) how about you? You should have this soup while you are telling the story."

Mr. Bay responds to his wife with a smile, "Yes, Minh Oi, I would."

Gulping down the soup, he enjoys the freshness of chicken. Mr. Bay begins with what he knew about his father's life. The oldest memory he recalls is when Mr. Ngoc and Mr. Ngoc's uncle, Mr. Khan, both bravely escaped out of China into Viet Nam. While he enjoys his daughter in-law's cooking, Mr. Ngoc listens to his son; he is pleased with the way his son tells the story. Mr. Bay always is a gifted storyteller. He starts with Mr. Ngoc's journey.

Chapter 1
Where the Past Began

It is the year 1891. Side by side, the lands of China and Viet Nam seamlessly connect, defying the political borders of man.

As the moon rises just above the hill, the silhouettes of two people can be seen. One is Mr. Khan, a man of about thirty years and the other is Mr. Khan's nephew, Truong Ngoc, now a little boy of roughly eleven years.

Both quietly walk alongside each other like ghosts through the jungle full of fierce beasts. Many months they walk on silk slippers, surviving on anything they can. At last, they escape from China and cross the border into Viet Nam country. The end of their journey finds them scratched and scarred, but alive.

As strangers in a new is land, without a job and without a roof over their heads, the only way they know to make a living is to continue rooster fighting and win money.

Truong Ngoc's parents have long since passed away. It is Mr. Khan whose caring love and devotion have helped to guide his young nephew. Over the years, their relationship has become closer to one of father and son. With such affection, Truong Ngoc worships the ground on which his uncle walks. For many years, they travel together, drifting from northern to southern Viet Nam. Mr. Ngoc grows into a handsome young man and soon meets his first wife who gives him two sons. Finding success in rooster gambling, Mr. Ngoc and his uncle purchase many acres of rice paddy land.

Every day, Mrs. Ngoc takes care of her husband's rice paddy business while Mr. Ngoc and Mr. Khan are out gambling. Mr. Khan controls Mr. Ngoc, because of that Mr. Ngoc was very tighfisted with his wife. Mr. Khan constantly criticizes everything Mrs. Ngoc does and she feels unable to satisfy her father in-law. Mr. Khan's influence on his nephew is overwhelming and Mr. Ngoc finds himself too weak to defend his wife. Over time, Mrs. Ngoc feels regretful, and her hatred of both her husband and Mr. Khan intensifies.

Mrs. Ngoc's mind soon becomes damaged from her mistreatment. Despite this harm, Mr. Ngoc remains unaware that his wife's feelings have been deeply hurt.

One day, Mr. Ngoc and his uncle arrive home earlier than usual. They quietly walk into the house without Mrs. Ngoc noticing their entrance. When Mr. Ngoc breathlessly dashes down to the kitchen looking for food, he sees his wife sprinkle powder into two of the rice pudding bowls. Trying to remain unnoticed, Mr. Ngoc silently goes back up to the front part of the house and gulps down air. Once recovered, he returns to the kitchen, acting as if he had just walked in, and compliments his wife's beauty. Unfamiliar with this show of affection or its intent, the action torments Mrs. Ngoc into a mix of feelings. She hesitates for a split second, but, remembering her purpose, carries on her plan.

As she hands over the bowl of rice pudding, Mr. Ngoc gazes longingly into his wife's eyes as he opens the palm of his hand to receive it. His memories of the fighting are bitter and he suddenly feels overwhelmed with the situation. A sharp pain is plunged into his heart, the hurt of it making him dizzy as the bowl tilts and pudding cascades onto the floor. Mr. Ngoc forgets that the dog stands nearby waiting for a treat. Instead of Mr. Ngoc dying from his wife's poison, the poor dog dies for its owner.

Later, Mr. Ngoc reveals the circumstance to his uncle. He calmly takes his wife in the canoe, paddles her across the river and sadly says goodbye. Her lover, a worker on their land, waits for her at the other side of the river's edge. Both of their sons remain with Mr. Ngoc.

Chapter 2
Heavy Burden on the Young Son

Over the next few years later, Mr. Ngoc again finds happiness with his second wife, Mrs. Ho Thiet. Her ancestors had traveled with the warriors from China into Viet Nam and settled in the northern mountains. Experts in Kung Fu, they fought in many battles and survived. Mrs. Ho Thiet ran away from her very unkind and controlling first husband. She separated from her family and drifted from the northern mountains to South Viet Nam.

It is there that she crosses paths with Mr. Ngoc, a man opposite to her in many ways. Mr. Ngoc is six feet tall, a soft spoken and quiet person (quite unlike her previous husband) while Mrs. Ho Thiet is a small and tough woman. With her strong mind and warrior-like ways, Mr. Khan is no longer able to rule the household nor push her around as he did to Mr. Ngoc's first wife. Instead of proving to be a heartless man, he very much loves her as a daughter and feels that what she does is right.

Because of old age, Mr. Khan gets ill and passes away. Mr. Ngoc experiences great sorrow with his uncle's death. He feels the lonesomeness most intensely, especially while gambling. Mr. Ngoc loses everything that he and his uncle had won and owed more to the winner.

To pay his debt, he pawns Bay, the older son of his second wife. Bay must work for seven years for the person to whom Mr. Ngoc lost.

Only then will Bay be released. Mr. Ngoc also becomes a rent collector for the new owner.

Bay, though young at ten years old, is very embittered toward his father, knowing that he must pay his father's debt. Frail and silent, he packs a few of his clothes and says goodbye to his mother, "Mother, I'm going."

Mrs. Ho Thiet loves her son very much but knows her son must go or her husband will face jail time.

Bay's job is to take care of the children of Dien Chu (the title of the rice paddy's owner). He must take them to the school and watch over them. Everyday, Bay sits outside the window looking into the classroom and learns how to read and write by himself. He takes a stick and writes on banana leaves or on the dust. Three months pass by until the teacher notices and approaches Bay, asking, "Why don't you come in?"

Unashamedly, Bay answers, "I'm a servant; I have no gold to pay you."

The good-hearted teacher responds, "Come in and learn. There is no need to pay me."

Bay walks into the classroom and sits in the corner of the dusty floor, following the lesson while enduring spiteful looks from the children. The children begin to get jealous and tell their parents a few months later. When the boss finds out, he sends Bay to work in the rice paddy fields and no longer allows him to care for the children.

Bay's absence makes the teacher concerned about him. The teacher searches for Bay all over the village, causing gossip among the villagers. However, Bay is found quickly. The teacher hands Bay a notebook written by his own hand. He says to Bay, "Read this notebook and practice your hand writing, then come to see me when you can. It doesn't matter what time. I'll wait for you." Bay is grateful for the teacher's kindness and bows his head to show his respect.

Bay has to practice writing under the moonlight or reading in dim light every time he gets a chance. He wants his writing to be as beautiful as his teacher's writing in the notebook. While everyone is asleep at night, Bay goes to see his teacher. Unfortunately, his secret is discovered by another servant, who tattletales to Dien Chu. Dien Chu immediately looks for him. When he finds Bay, he tells him, "I forbid you to go to school while you are my servant. You must be punished."

Dien Chu takes a water buffalo tail hanging on the wall and begins to whip Bay's back, his hand coming down in forceful lashes. The roughness of the water buffalo tail breaks in to Bay's skin, as Dien Chu yells with every stroke, "Don't you ever forget your place!"

The harsh sentence leaves many scars across Bay's back. Mrs. Ho Thiet is shocked when she visits and sees her son wounded, so that she attempts to use her Kung Fu to give Dien Chu back some of what he did to her sons. But Bay convinces his mother not to seek revenge. He says, "It is not the time mother. I am all right. Our time will come. Seven years will be very quick. Go home mother; tell father not to worry. His debt soon will be pay off. Please! Don't come back, stay home and wait for me."

Mrs. Ho Thiet respects her son's wish. Swallowing her anger, she returns home. While holding back tears, she pounds against her chest and screams at Mr. Ngoc, "For the rest of your life, I forbid you to gamble! Dien Chu has beaten our son badly today. I did not bring him into this world for someone else to use him and strike him that way!"

Mr. Ngoc feels remorseful after his wife's testimony and becomes an even quieter man than he was before. Meanwhile, Bay works harder and harder, waiting for the contract to reach its full term.

Seven years pass. Mr. Ngoc is finally able to take the contract paper to the village court, proving his son's time as a servant has ended. Dien Chu releases his son. Bay feels free, as if he has a set of wings growing on his back. Immediately, the young man reunites with his parents.

Chapter 3
Wrongful Trust

At that point in time, Viet Nam had been under the control of French for the past hundred years. French soldiers often came into the village, raping and killing many Vietnamese people. In addition, Cambodian Khmer people came quickly to hack off the heads of Vietnamese people with their machetes.

Bay receives an order from the Viet Minh commanding him to beat the drums and warn the villagers whenever French troops get close by. Since he had just been released from slavery a short time ago, Bay is eager to do his new duty.

When he is first aware of the French in the village, he uses all his strength to pound the drums with strong muscular arms developed from working in the rice paddies. The Viet Minh promised to tell him if the French get too close, allowing him time to flee. The drum sounds intoxicate Bay like rice wine as he batters them.

Unfortunately, Bay wrongly places trust in the Viet Minh promise. Bay is only conscious that the French soldiers are nearby when a duck falls from the sky before his very eyes, its life taken by the bullet of a gun. Bay tosses his drumsticks to the side and quickly runs off.

He hides among the tall cattail grass that grew in the water stream. Although Bay is out off sight, he can still hear the screaming and bombardment of gunfire. Many times he wants to turn back to fight, but realizes there is no way to help anyone. His strong arms and bare hands cannot combat the whole troop of French soldiers or savage

Cambodian Khmer machetes. Bay runs far away from his village until he no longer hears the screams and the shooting. He searches for his family, but they are nowhere in sight. While he is moving forward in the waterway, unexpectedly, he collides accidentally with a young woman. She had hidden herself inside the tall cattail grass under the water. To Bay, she looks afraid, like a lost kitten. Bay pulls her hand and leads the way.

Following the stream, the tall cattail grass covers them as they move; both are safe from the French and Cambodian Khmer for now. They pass many rice paddies on both side of the creek. They eat the roots of cattail grass to fill their hunger. It is a miracle when both of their families end up in the same village, Dien Ba Lat.

After being reunited with their families, Bay and Danh, the young woman, go their separate ways. They continue with life, trying to earn their living by working for other rice paddies' owners.

Most of South Viet Nam's natural surroundings are wetlands and jungle. The people are poor. Their clothing is made of rough burlap fabrics. They take the ashes from burned wood, put it in a bucket and add rain water. After a good stir, they let it sit for about a month. The ashes settle at the bottom of the bucket. The clear liquid at the top becomes their shampoo.

War is always happening in Viet Nam, generation to generation. They have forgotten peace even exists. In spite of this challenge, Mrs. Ho Thiet knows her son needs a wife and goes to ask the Matchmaker to find three young girls his age. The Matchmaker shortly returns and tells Mrs. Ho Thiet she has found suitable candidates seventeen to eighteen years of age. She suggests to Mrs. Ho Thiet to plan a day to spy on them.

All three of the young girls are asked to carry logs that Bay has cut into the Matchmaker's house. The purpose is to see which girl is fastest. Danh, the girl Bay led out of the danger zone, happens to be one of the three. Being very small, but quick on her feet, she wins Mrs. Ho Thiet's attention. Perhaps this is because Ho Thiet too, is physically petite in size. Mrs. Ho Thiet's next step is to set up an opportunity for her son to secretly see Danh.

After working hard out in the rice paddies all day, Danh lies on a hammock, taking her nap. Bay tiptoes from his hiding place behind the trees to where the hammock hangs. Bay is surprised when he recognizes the young woman as the same one who ran with him in the last French attack.

She has been on his mind. The last time he saw her, he felt nothing other than the will to survive. Now, his heart beats like a drum. He is very happy his mother chose this young woman. He has never quite forgotten her long dark hair, her light brown skin, her baby face and her heart shape lips. Standing before her, a moment longer, he takes a deep breath, and then quietly walks away with a smile.

Sensing someone watching her, Danh barely dares to open her eyes. Then, she shuts them as tightly as she can. Her heart beats so fast, and its thumps sound to Danh like the pounding of the harvest rice under the moonlight.

Immediately upon realizing Bay has gone, she rushes off to find her mother, Mrs. Duong. Mrs. Duong explains to her daughter that Bay's parents have proposed a marriage. Danh obeys her parents, unaware that her future husband is the same man who helped her escape from the last French attack. In the culture of Viet Nam, the first meeting is termed "Dam Hoi." A few months later, the "Dam Cuoi" wedding follows.

Mrs. Ho Thiet prepares traditional gifts: clothes for Danh, tea for her parents and some rice cakes. Mrs. Ho Thiet calls the entire family members to help with the wedding. Each person carries one gift in his or her hand. In front of the house of Mrs. Duong's relative, the wedding party forms a straight line in single file, so they can all enter slowly, respectfully, one by one.

Since Danh and Bay's families are newly settled in the village, they're homeless. They drift between households to work and camp outside at dark.

Light shines from the moon on clear nights, helping the newlywed couple dig a hole in the rice straw stack. It creates shelter, almost like an igloo. They crawl inside to sleep.

With everyone working hard, before too long the family is able to buy some land and build their home. Mr. and Mrs. Duong move back to Mrs. Duong's old village after their daughter marries Bay.

Unfortunately, the past catches up with them. Bay's previous village learns where Bay's family lives. People in the prior village disliked

Mr. Ngoc, Bay's father, since rent collectors are often unsympathetic to the people. The rumors fly to the new settlement, making more enemies than friends for Bay's family.

While Bay's sister is out with her husband, the Viet Minh tie them up and cut her pregnant stomach open. The baby of five months dies as she does. Her husband's head is cut off. Their bodies lay together in a canoe attached at the river dock. One of the Viet Minh paddles the canoe by the house and yells up at the shore, "Truong Ngoc, go to the town waterfront, pick up your daughter and her husband. You had a grandchild. It's a boy."

Bay and his brothers bring their sister's body, her husband's and the child's body home. They try to swallow the anger coursing though them. It is a hard thing to do when there is no justice. Never until this moment has Bay thought to betray his country, but with this complex circumstance, he feels desperate. Bay evaluates the situation carefully. On one hand, Viet Minh is his native government. But, they're killers. The community always must prove they are faithful to the Viet Minh; the anxiety of this pressure is constantly in their daily life. Since the beginning of their control, the Viet Minh have influenced people to go against each other, to spy on one another. They live a life of fear, always worrying about doing something wrong and trusting no one, even anyone they thought would be their friend.

On the other hand, French troops often come to the village; Bay can see them clearly out in the open. Either way, the death sentence hangs over their heads. In order to survive, Bay must depart completely from his lifestyle under the Viet Minh. He knows disloyalty to his country is punishable by death. Nevertheless, his family members have already died for other reasons. He is no longer living in peace and quiet.

After thinking it through thoroughly, seventeen year old Bay decides to go to the city. He pretends that he is going for things he needs and to see what is going on in the city. Instead, he walks into the French headquarters to enlist and is sworn in. He makes a deal with the French that they must take some troops and come into the village to set everyone in his family free. Because of what he went through as a young boy, Bay became tough, and now leadership shows on his face. The French commander keeps his promise and puts Bay in charge of a group of Vietnamese soldiers.

They arrive at the edge of the river. Viet Minh begin to shoot. Meanwhile, Bay paddles a canoe across the river and secretly rescues his family. Everyone has to leave everything behind and run for their lives. In this frantic moment, Danh manages to grab one of the chickens and takes it with her.

Bay takes his family to the hometown of Danh's mother. Luckily, the French agree for Bay to be stationed at Danh's village, Cay Gua. Bay's life begins a new chapter.

Chapter 4
Children

The danger is finally past for the time being. Now they can all focus their attention on getting a first-born son and grandchild in the family. Mr. Ngoc and Mrs. Ho demand of Danh, "You must get pregnant soon. We want a grandson."

Danh smiles with happiness as she answers her in-law, "I'll do just that Mother and Father."

The couple does not have difficulty in succeeding. When Danh is first pregnant, Mr. Ngoc is happy, fully believing it will be a boy. He prays and prays and prays to God and to his ancestors for a boy. He says, "A firstborn boy would make the family be stronger. The boy will take care of the family just like my son Bay does."

Mr. Ngoc is pleased with the answer. His first grandchild is indeed a boy. One month after the baby was born, they celebrate with a big party to welcome him into the world. Fruits are set upon tables for the ancestors and outside for God to express their family's gratitude. All the villagers are invited. The baby brings joy to their life. Sadly, the baby cries so much, he drinks little of milk from his mother. Three months and ten days later the baby dies.

Danh is soon pregnant again. Mrs. Duong makes sure her daughter is in good health while her daughter is carrying a child. She finds many good foods for Danh to consume. Her infant comes into the world crying like his brother before him. There are no Western doctors to consult, only a midwife and Chinese herbalist. They do all they can, but this child too dies at exactly three months and ten days of age.

The villagers begin to gossip. Seriously superstitious, they believe Danh's sons are Con Ranh Con Lon, one soul that keeps coming back after a short period. They tell Bay to cut his dead son in half, to put both parts back together and bury the body.

The disappointment appears on the faces of Danh's parents in-law. Danh also must put up with gossip. Family members and neighbors whisper unkind words behind her back and the gossip flies through the village households. Night and day Danh is reminded of the rebirth of the child's soul. She swallows harsh words without showing her emotion. She knows that despite the ruthless murmurs, they are harmless. The villagers are just showing their concern; they just express their good intentions in the wrong way. Moreover, she knows if she ever needs anyone's help, none of them would ever let her down.

A year later, Danh delivers a very pretty girl, but one with a problem. A line runs across her belly, as if she too has been mended back together. Again, the villagers blather, and try to convince Bay that his daughter is a reincarnation of her brother's soul. The baby cries and cries. When they call in a Witch doctor to use magical powers to save the child, it is hopeless. She dies like her two brothers, at three months and ten days of a mysterious illness.

The couple finds this death even more agonizingly painful. Bay feels much heartache for his wife. Often, he takes her out to the rice paddies to ride on buffalo backs, play the flute and hunt their food. Bay spends as much time as he can with his wife so she can be far away from the blabbermouths. Yet he knows the danger of Viet Minh is always nearby. He whispers into his wife's ear, "Minh Oi, things will get better." Their love of each other grows stronger by the day. It is easy for Danh to conceive. Once again, she is expecting a child.

Mrs. Duong spends extra time pampering her during the pregnancy. It is very important for her daughter's happiness. Mrs. Duong looks up at the sky every night with burning incense and calls upon God and on her ancestors spirits, "God, Grandparents, Mother and Father, please watch over my daughter and my grandchild. And please, let it be boy."

Danh and Bay too beg for their forebears' spirits to help. Both try to keep away from scandalmongers and relatives. It is uncomfortable for to carry this baby. It is a long nine months and ten days. Bay is different from most of other men. He never curses or disrespects anyone. With his wife, he is also very gentle, but as a soldier, he is a warrior. Danh can feel her husband's love wrapping around her. He seals her inside his heart, distracting Danh from all the gossips. At last, the time comes. Danh tells her husband, "I think I'll have the baby tonight."

Mrs. Ho Thiet hears her daughter- in-law and quickly rushes toward Bay, saying, "Let's go Bay! We have to pick up Mrs. Lan!"

Going swiftly out of the door, Bay and his mother head toward their river dock and untie the canoe. Bay paddles to the next village where Mrs. Lan's residence lies. They know they must hurry before the baby is born. When they arrive at the Midwife's house, fog has already covered the jungle. It looks like a giant white blanket wrapped about a giant beast with them trapped inside. Still about a hundred feet away from Mrs. Lan's house, Mrs. Ho Thiet yells out to the Midwife, "Mrs. Lan! Mrs. Lan!"

Mrs. Lan asks, "Who is there?"

Again, Mrs. Ho Thiet hollers loudly, "This is Ho Thiet! Bay and I have come to get you!"

Bay too shouts, "My baby is about to be born. We need your help!"

Inside her bungalow, Mrs. Lan grabs her pack and dashes out of the door. It isn't easy to get through the overgrown bushes, rapidly as they push them to the side, making a path to the river. Mrs. Ho Thiet carries a rice straw torch so they can see their way home. Mrs. Lan steps down into the canoe and signals Mrs. Ho Thiet to hand over the torch. She sits in the middle and raises the torch above her head to light the river. Mrs. Ho Thiet sits in front to help her son row the canoe. Bay releases the loop on the dock. Without delay he hops into the back and steers the canoe forward.

The darkness of the jungle is unfriendly to everyone. Soldiers forbid anyone wandering outside after dark. But Bay has no choice. The situation is too grave to spend time analyzing or being afraid of if the Viet Minh will shoot. Beside, animals are beginning to hunt for their prey. Red eyes show through the pitch black night and they know something on shore is watching them.

The owls hoot with their human-like faces. Vietnamese people believe owls are the devil's messengers; their whooping call brings dread to people. An owl seen on top of someone's roof is a sign of bad luck or failure to come.

Yet even with these frightening creatures surrounding them, Bay is fearless. He is accustomed to days and nights admits jungle life. Without difficulty, he guides his mother and Mrs. Lan safety to shore.

Bay ties the canoe to the dock, takes the burning torch from Mrs. Lan, and leads the way to his house. Inside, Danh has contractions and the baby comes close to birth. This child will be her fourth. Mrs. Duong puts a piece of cloth into her daughter's mouth and whispers into her daughter's ear, "Don't scream. It's unladylike."

Danh listens to her mother, even in painful labor. It is difficult, but she controls herself and sinks her teeth down into the cloth. One of her hands grabs her mother's hand, and the other grabs her mother in-law's. The women take complete control over the situation. Noticing Bay still standing nearby, Mrs. Ho Thiet orders, "Bay, get out!"

Men are forbidden to be present while women give birth. So Bay has no choice other than go up in front of the house with the rest of the family.

Mrs. Lan quickly examines Danh and says, "Now push, Danh!"

Danh gathers all her strength to push her baby out of the womb. After a few pushes, the baby's head emerges out from the birth canal. Mrs. Lan pulls the baby out from Danh and announces, "It's a baby girl."

Even with their disappointment, because it is not a boy, Danh's mother in-law and her mother still express their gratefulness to God and their ancestors for keeping Danh safe during labor. Together they go outside and bow their heads to the ground.

With a history of babies dying in the family, they postpone naming Danh's newborn daughter. She cries like all the others. Bay marks the surface of the pole at front of their house to keeping track of the days. The time of three months rapidly approaches, and now it seems they are waiting for the baby to die.

In a bitter voice, Mrs. Ho Thiet tells her son, "Bay, prepare wood for the coffin." But Bay refused. He tiredly repeats to his mother, "Mother, I'll do it when the time calls."

While everyone else gives up hope, Danh and Bay embrace their baby every day, and walk out to the rice paddies to speak to God. They think if they are out in the open, perhaps their request could be better hear. They say, "God, from above and beyond, with your worldly vision, please shine down on us. We have never done anything wrong. We beg you to let our daughter remain with us." In this way, they repeatedly pray.

Soft winds drift by, gently, giving the baby a breath of fresh air. With the poems whispered in Danh and Bay's voices, the baby relaxes. She even agrees to drink more milk from her mother. Both implore their infant, "Please stay on this earth with us. Don't leave us. We love you and need you. You're our strength."

Days go by fast. Danh's tears drop on her daughter, frequently. She holds onto her baby and gives all her love to the child, hoping this moment will last forever.

Chapter 5
Khmer Woman Saved a Child

On the first of the last ten days, a Cambodian woman walks by the house. She hears the baby crying and walks in without invitation to ask, "Can I see the child?"

Unexpectedly, seeing the total stranger inside their house, both parents are so desperate to save their child, they instantly answer, "Yes! Please save my child."

They are willing to try anything, even if the stranger may be one of the savage beasts, a Khmer Woman.

However, the woman appears to be a monk. When this is revealed, it relieves Bay and Danh from their unpleasant thoughts. They believe no harm will come to them, that a good thing is forthcoming. The woman instructs someone to place the baby outside the three passageways. Mrs. Khanh, a wife of Bay's brother, is to pretend she is walking by, finding a little girl whom someone had abandoned.

Mrs. Khanh runs back into the house, screaming and pointing her finger in the direction of the baby, "There is a baby! Poor, baby! Someone threw a baby away!"

Mrs. Khanh grabs Danh's hand and pulls her to the passageway. Danh also acts as if this is the first time she has seen her baby. Excitedly, she yells out for her husband and others nearby. With everyone in the family shouting, soon the entire neighborhood runs out to witness the event. This stops the devils from coming to claim the baby's soul before the monk can bless the child.

Mrs. Khanh lays the baby into a bamboo basket and passes her through the dog entrance. The monk uses her magical powers and skills to fight off the evil sprits. She orders Mr. Khanh to take five incenses and burn them on the top middle of the baby's head. Several years later, that dime-sized scar would still be visible, as it would be visible on all her siblings and all her cousins to come. After the ceremony, the monk weaves a white threaded necklace for the baby. She tells Danh the baby is actually her second child, the child she has been searching everywhere to find, for so long. The monk becomes the girl's Master of Spirit, and says the baby's soul is forever connected to the world of the supernatural. She gives Danh a little bottle filled with pills tiny as a needle's tip. Danh is instructed to give her baby one every night at bed time. They must remember to take the baby out daily to beg for milk from women in the village to prove to the devils that she is from the unwanted. Though it is pretending, the devils are fooled.

The Villagers and everyone in the family, including the child's parents, all think God sent the monk. They name the baby Luom (which means, "Pick up trash"), and prohibit Luom from calling her mother Me (Mother). Instead, she must call her mother Vu (Nanny). From then on Luom sleeps peacefully and so does everyone else. Her Master of Spirit promises to come back in one year to visit. She never returns.

As complicated as their lives had been, it finally feels as if a dark cloud has passed. Their life begins to shine just as bright as the sun outside. Bay receives orders from the Army that he must move. They are sending him off to new location. It takes all day for the family to travel along the bumpy road to his new station.

As the troops begin to move, the uneven road cause the truck to bounce. Luom is unable to get her daily naps. When the truck stops, the soldiers worry about being ambushed by the Viet Minh and Khmer people. The crying infant creates enormous mental strain, and finally the soldiers are no longer able to handle their cool. They make a suggestion to Bay. Perhaps he could find what he considers the best location, probably a place without too many bushes and trees, so he and his soldiers could see far in the distance to look out for their enemies. There, Luom can sleep.

Soldiers stand guard on both sides of the road. Some patrol up and down the road while others remove the hammock from the truck. They stretch it from the rear of their truck to the front of Luom's truck. Danh rests with Luom on the hammock and sings her baby to sleep. No one else dares to make a sound. They tiptoe around as if Luom is an infant princess. Luckily, nothing happens while they are stopped, and their journey continues after an hour of waiting for their Princess to fully rest.

Sergeant Bay is station in Ca Mau for three years, allowing a quiet time for his family. Then he must again move to Vinh Binh Hemet. It isn't easy on Danh, who is pregnant for the fifth time.

Shortly after, they settle in the village of Vinh Binh. Danh gives Luom a little sister with big round black eyes. They jokingly call her "car headlights." Beside the thick hair on top of her head, her body is also the hairiest. Her second nickname is, "Monkey baby", even though she is actually very healthy, chubby and cute. She is the epitome of wellness and happiness. Everyone in the compound adores her. She is as different from Luom as day is to night. She is always playful, eats well, and seldom cries. She smiles constantly and her white skin is decidedly dissimilar from Luom's darker complexion. Few Vietnamese people are born with skin as white as Luom's sister's. She is treated like an angel princess. They all believe she is Bay's angel— his military promotion comes the night after she is born. The wives of other soldiers who come to play with Luom's sister never forget to tell Bay that she is his good luck charm. They name her Thu Huong (which means, "Fall fragrant").

Chapter 6
A Child Saved Her Family

While Thu Huong draws attention from everyone around her, Luom feels abandoned by her parents. Instead of playing with the other children, she begins to demand her mother's time. Luom clings to Mrs. Danh tightly, nagging and annoying her.

The soldiers' families' lives are separate from the outside world. The compound is in the middle of nowhere. Other than going to the market, which is open only for a few hours in the mornings in town nearby, there is nothing else to do. In 1954, the rural area of Vinh Binh is wetlands, surrounded for miles by only rice paddies and covered with massive tropical trees.

One day Luom, now four years old, says to her father, "Please Father! Close the compound gate! Please!"

"Why would you want to close the gate?"

Again, Luom pleads, "Please Father! Close the gate please!""No Luom."

Luom throws a tantrum. Unable to control her temper, she screams at her father, "Father, close the gate! I told you to close the gate! Why don't you do what I ask you?"

Sgt. Bay becomes irritated with his daughter and angry about her disrespectful words. He tells Luom, "Give me a reason you want to cage us in. You must want me to whip your bottom?"

Fearless even in the face of her father's threat, Luom continues, "Do you want Viet Minh and Khmer to come in and chop our heads off? I don't want to die yet."

Those listening feel a chill down their spines at the sobbing and hysterical words of four year old Luom to her father. It is not right for a child to speak this way to her elder. But other than this outburst, Luom is normally quiet. When the soldiers overhear Sgt. Bay and Luom exchange words, they too begin to question why Luom is acting this way.

Without the order given by Sgt. Bay, the soldiers line up for a head count, making certain everyone is present. The soldier who is second in commander of the compound orders a few others to go out and bring back the patrols. Head counts are not usually done without Sgt. Bay's order. A few of them darkly curse Luom. However, others remain silent, deep in thought. During Luom's fit, it is difficult for the families with children, who must explain the meaning of head counts to their younger ones and why they must do what Luom wants.

The next day Luom cries again and begs that the gate be closed. In order to stop Luom from crying, they close the gate. Finally Sgt. Bay and all of his men decide, if Luom still cries after the fifth night, she will be punished for "crying wolf."

But Luom does not let them rest peacefully on the fifth night. Around three in the afternoon, she asks them to lock up the gate, two hours earlier than usual. Once again they argue with her, but she wins with her tears. Everyone thought it would bring her tears to an end when she had her own way.

Yet she is unstoppable and persist wailing, "Viet Minh!! Viet Minh and Khmer are going to kill all of us."

Sgt. Bay, disturbed by his daughter's words asks, "What do you mean Viet Minh are going to kill us?"

Luom repeats her shrill scream, "Viet Minh will come and kill us!"

It is clear that Luom is bursting with fear because of strong superstitious beliefs held by Sgt. Bay and his soldiers. They all begin to have an unsettled feeling. The men shake their heads and said is pointless to attempt to quiet her as she cries and screams. Now they've done everything they possibly could, from sweet talk to threats, but Luom is still screaming, repeating the same words and refusing to eat. Finally exhausted, she passes out.

While Luom sleeps, the people all gather together and express their concern: what if Viet Minh really come as Luom predicted? What do they have to do? And the answer is: to be alert. They certainly could not go to the French and say, "The little child just warned us from her nightmare."

Still, few took note of what the little child had warned. They all went to bed, leaving only one man on guard.

Fog clothed the moon. The jungle fills with fireflies. Night creatures are out for their prey. The howls of beasts, grating legs of crickets and hoarse calls of frogs, quickly become a concert of terror, making the jungle even more horrible than usual, daring anyone to step from beyond safe boundaries.

Disregarding the cacophony, one brave shadow appears, moving quickly under the gloomy sky. His movements are blurry like an apparition as he heads toward the compound. Meanwhile, the lonely soldier in the watchtower begins to drift to sleep in the chill, fresh air above the dense foliage. He leaves his duty behind as dreaming takes him.

All of a sudden, Luom awakens from her nightmare and shrieks at the top of her lungs, "Viet Minh! Viet Minh!" Her voice is horrifying. It echoes through the murky jungle. Her body trembles as if she will go to pieces. Her eyes are wide open. The sound rouses her father and all others in the compound. Again and again her parents try to calm her, but the more they try, the more frightened she becomes.

Superstition grabs a hold of Sgt. Bay. He suddenly feels that something awful is about to happen. Remembering the time his daughter asked him to close the gate, Sgt. Bay's spine tingles with the threat of danger. Startled and with searching eyes, Bay hiding the worry in his mind, speaks to his wife, "I'm going up the tower." Grabbing a flashlight and a grenade, Sgt. Bay climbs to the top of the look out.

In the meantime, the flitting shadow moves closer to the gate. Although disturbed by Luom's high-pitched voice, he refuses to stop. He is determined to accomplish his mission.

Sgt. Bay reaches the viewing location. He immediately spots a barefoot man, wearing only shorts, his head wrapped in dark bandanas. He is carrying a big clear glass bomb. Sgt. Bay can see the explosive inside it, he realizes in a split second that his enemy is down at the bottom of the tower. The man cannot be allowed any closer.

Without a second thought, Sgt. Bay takes aim at the man. The grenade flies out of Sgt. Bay's hand, falling to land at the man's foot, followed by a huge noise. The man's body is blown to pieces and the tower's bottom wall collapses. All is soundless for a moment, as if time stands still. An agonizing moment. Sgt. Bay yells out to his men down below, "Cac anh em co sao khong?" Is everyone ok?

When no one answers, he is sure that all his men at the bottom are dead. He hopes his family on the second floor is safe.

Outside, a group of Viet Minh scurries toward the compound, yelling "Tien len, tien len anh em dong chi! Forward, forward comrades!

Sgt. Bay calls out for his wife to help, "Minh oi! Bring me ammunition!"

Danh, hearing the enemy roaring fire, knows she must help her husband in order to stay alive. She quickly tells Luom to hold Thu Huong. At this point Luom is no longer crying, but she is terrified and frozen in place. In spite of seeing that her daughter is in dreadfully state, there are no other alternatives; she leaves the children where they are.

Gathering all the items that her husband requested, Danh carries some on her shoulders and some in her hands, taking as much as she could. In a flash Danh's motherly appearance vanishes. She had transformed into a woman-warrior. Danh climbs up the ladder to the lookout tower. Now exposed to the outside and visible to her enemies, Danh is in danger. When she reaches the top, the situation forces her to stay in the battle side by side with her husband. Husband and wife and the awakened tower guard fight for their lives.

When the shooting stops for a moment, Sgt. Bay takes advantage of this and lets his wife go back to their children. Unfortunately, as soon as her foot touches the stepladder, the Viet Minh spot her and begin shooting. Sgt. Bay fires back to help his wife arrive safely below.

Danh is blessed by God. She makes it back to their daughters in one piece. As she pulls them toward her in a protective embrace, suddenly the ceiling collapses in the place where the children were sitting. Danh's hands shiver as she tries to keep the children in her arms. She said, "Thank you God and Buddha, you saved their lives."

Outside, drums and tin cans are bashed together, louder and

louder. They use a mega phone to call out, "Sgt. Bay, listen! We are the people from the North, come to set free all people of the South from French invasion. Give up your guns and surrender!"

Barrages of bullets follow these repeated shouts over and over. In spite of the attack, Sgt. Bay remains calm. He is the king of his castle. He will not give up and he continues to hold out. The sound of battle is heard at the next army post. Although they are concerned, it is too dangerous to go out in the middle of the night to risk their lives for anyone.

At 9:00 the next morning, French and Vietnamese troops march in to rescue them. But no rescuing is need. Long before dawn, the Viet Minh withdrew from the battle, unsuccessful in taking over. Happy with the victory, the big French commander lifts Sgt. Bay up into the air, proclaiming him a First Lieutenant. The soldier who had fallen asleep on the job becomes Lieutenant Bay's right-hand man. Lieutenant Bay is not happy with his promotion because he considers himself and others lucky to be alive. He believes God saved their lives. Now that the danger is over, Lieutenant Bay has time to draw into his own mind. He realized the French military action was extremely delayed even though they knew his post was vulnerable. He realizes he can no longer depend on French support. He will have to gain more knowledge to defend his post in the future. He did not blame the nearby Vietnamese post for failing to make any attempt to help him. Perhaps, Lieutenant Bay thinks, they face the same problem. If the situation had been reversed, he might have done the same. The other Vietnamese soldiers are no different from him: they all have to survive. If they do not stay in the military, their life will become very difficult as it was before. At least by joining in the French, they are helping save their own lives and the lives of their love ones. Yet, their lives still remain under a dark cloud.

Chapter 7
War Damages a Young Child's Mind

The bodies of the dead are buried; a group of new soldiers and their families come to replace them. As for Lieutenant Bay and his family, they try to recover from the battle. Luom's mind seems to have suffered the most from the encounter. She spends most of her time staring at the walls and distances herself from everyone. Worried, her parents send her to live with her grandmother. But Danh and Lieutenant Bay can't leave their post to take her. Luom must go with a group of strangers, soldiers who happen to be heading to Mrs. Duong's village. Like a zombie, Luom walks out of her parents' sight. No one can know the mind of this four year old child, in this moment.

The soldiers with whom Luom travels admire how brave she is. She just quietly munches on her dry rice Mrs. Danh packed for her. If she hears anything they say to her, she doesn't show it.

At last, the Army convoy reaches Mrs. Duong. The soldiers drop Luom off and then continue their journey. Mrs. Duong is happy to see her granddaughter, but disturbed at Luom's condition and the way she was delivered to her. There is no explanation from Danh. Mrs. Duong is unaware of what Luom has gone through, but she thought something terrible must have happened. Otherwise, her daughter never would have sent her granddaughter to her in this way.

Life with her grandmother is better for Luom, but only for the first few months. In the late afternoon, Mrs. Duong often spots Luom at the back door, seated, staring out at the pond. Luom stays silent, deep in thought. She has difficulty eating food and soon becomes ill. Luom just lies on her bed sometimes, or, with little energy, sits at the back door.

Mrs. Duong is concerned about her granddaughter. While she combs Luom's hair, the loving grandmother asks in soft tones, "Con co nho Vu con Khong? (Do you miss your Nanny?)

Still a small child, Luom is unfamiliar with what the word "miss" actually means. With a sad face, Luom says in baby talk, "Khong, Ba Ngoai. (No Grandmother)."

Dissatisfied with her granddaughter's answer and pausing the comb, Mrs. Duong searches for the truth behind her granddaughter's eyes. She knows the child doesn't understand the word "miss." She asks Luom, "Con co thuong Vu con khong?" (Do you love your Nanny?)

Luom nods her head repeatedly and answers in tears, "Da! Da! (*Yes! Yes!*)"

Mrs. Duong takes a deep breath and releases a small moan of worry. She tells one of her daughters to get Luom ready to go home. Luom gets up and begins to run about. She is thrilled and eats a lot that evening. With her granddaughter in high spirits, Mrs. Duong is overjoyed to see her come back to life. Luom asks Mrs. Duong, "Ba Ngoai, could I bring something home for my parents?"

"What do you want to bring with you?"

Overjoyed, Luom says to her grandmother, "Mmm…chicken."

Mrs. Duong's face shines as she looks at her granddaughter. "Then we must take one with us." Luom's eyes brighten when Mrs. Duong agrees and they both go to the barn for Luom to choose her bird. Luom picks the biggest chicken she sees. Excited about the following day, she goes to sleep imagining herself at home with her parents.

At four o'clock next morning, Luom and Mrs. Duong wake up, eat their breakfast and start their trip. The journey is not easy. Because Mrs. Duong is afraid of riding the bus, they must take the long route. First, they climb aboard the canoe and later transfer to the water buffalo wagon. Luom is full of energy. Mrs. Duong, on the other hand, feels worn out. At long last, they arrive at the compound to the happiness and surprise of Lieutenant Bay and Danh.

On her first evening home, Luom asks that her chicken be cooked to feed the entire group of twenty people in the compound.

There is no argument at her request, for her words spoken in the past have saved lives. All make sure the chicken rice soup is divided evenly so there would be enough to go around. A short time after Luom reunites with her parents, Lieutenant Bay receives another order from the military to move back to Ca Mau and live in military housing. Lieutenant Bay becomes a dog trainer for the French. As a reward, they give Lieutenant Bay a beautiful, white fluffy dog. It is name Kiki and quickly becomes Luom's pal.

Life in this compound is very exciting; the daily routine for the soldiers interests Luom. Every morning, she hears her uncle Khanh's bugle blown loudly to awaken the soldiers. The melodies are, "Thang nao thuc chua? Thang nao chua thuc? Thang nao thuc roi, thang nao ngoi day." (Who is awake and who is not. Who is wakening? And who is sitting here?) The same melodies repeated over and over for about 5 minutes. Luom races out of bed to make sure she is the first in line to receive food. Some of them ask, "Are you a soldier?"

Luom proudly nods her head, "Yes! I am."

Some think she is a spoiled child. Some think she is cute. Whatever anyone thinks, though, she knows that she is more comfortable with them than with children her own age.

Since the French military provides the food, they all receive cheese, bananas, bread and a cup of powdered milk (not typical Vietnamese food). Luom goes home, stores these away and looks to her father for breakfast money.

Luom, her sister Thu Huong, and KiKi head to the marketplace. Thu Huong and KiKi always must wait for Luom to buy her food first and then Luom insists that they buy whatever she bought. Strictly trained by her father, Luom's morning ritual never changes.

One morning, KiKi gets tired of waiting for Luom to make up her mind and decides to eat first. Lieutenant Bay becomes upset and whips its bottom, just as he would discipline his own daughters. From then on, never again did KiKi eat before Luom, Thu Huong or before they reached home. A short while later, having lived a full life, KiKi passes away. Luom refused to have another dog, knowing she would never forget KiKi.

Every afternoon, whether rain or shine, Luom goes to the mess hall and straight into the kitchen and asks the chef for the crunchy rice that sticks to the bottom of the pot. Tam Choi, Mrs. Danh's eighth sister, tops the crunchy rice with homemade coconut oil or pig fat, green onion, a sprinkle of salt and a little sugar. It is a delicious snack for everyone.

After nibbling their treats, Thu Huong and Luom run off to play near the pond at the front of their house. Thu Huong is fascinated with the plants that grow on top of the water. She stretches out her arm to take a floating water lily. Losing her balance, she falls into the pond and in a flash, sinks under the water. Panicking, Luom runs inside to tell her mother, but her tongue is stiff. There is no sound; Luom is voiceless. Even though Luom tries with all her strength, she remains mute. Finally, Luom pulls at her mother's hand and points to the pond where her sister's hair is floating on the surface. Mrs. Danh's eyes follow the direction of Luom's finger. When she sees the little spot of hair slowly sinking from the top of the water, she realizes it is Thu Huong. Mrs. Danh jumps into the pond and grabs Thu Huong's hair, bring Thu Huong out of the pond, desperately hoping she can bring her daughter back to life. She turns her daughter upside down, hits her on the back and all the water comes out from Thu Huong's stomach. She comes back life. Mrs. Danh believed Thu Huong must have blessed by God, and the messenger is Luom again.

Chapter 8
Life in The Swampland

End of Mr. Bay's story.

Luom's memories begin

Luom is just about too adjusted to the lifestyle in the city of Ca Mau, when she hears news that her father must relocate again. She asks, "Father, why do we always have to move? I like it here."

Lieutenant Bay patiently explains to his daughter, "We must move because the government is sending me. It is not me who wants to go."

Luom has to settle for her father's answer and help her parents pack up their belongings. As for Luom's aunt, she must return to Mrs. Duong.

The next morning they begin their journey. Luom's aunt goes to the bus station and the rest head down to the waterfront. Luom begins to have an uneasy feeling, about this passage. Although she usually loves to look at the water dancing about the boat, instead she is quiet and stares at it with empty thought.

The soldiers' compound is located across the river from Cai Nuoc, a small village in the middle of the swampland. The market is small and so is the population. They are all fishermen. During the night, the locals become Viet Minh. They burn beeswax lamps and torches, as many as they can gather, and form a line along on their side of the river. Then they bang pots, drums, and tin cans and use the megaphone to call the soldiers to surrender. Women and children run for shelter to avoid bullets and grenades.

Unfortunately, the protective shelter is only about a hundred feet away. Night after night, Mrs. Danh carries her younger daughter Thu Huong in one hand and grasps Luom with the other, running with them to the safety. Sometimes Luom is awake and aware of what is going on. Other times, Mrs. Danh yanks Luom out of bed without warning while she sleeps peacefully. Luom's body falls to the ground and her mother has to half drag her into the safety zone. Luom holds her mother's hand tightly, saying, "Vu dung buong tay con nhe," (Nanny, don't let go of my hand.)

In these dreadful situations, Mrs. Danh calms her daughter's nervousness and answers, "No! Nanny will never let your hand go. Don't you worry, baby."

One night, when Mrs. Danh is pulling Luom along too quickly, their hands slip apart. Luom is screams out, "Nanny! Nanny, you promised!"

Scared, and wandering in darkness as black as ink, her pants soaking wet, Luom screeches repeatedly, "Nanny! Nanny where are you Nanny!"

It is not easy to find each other. When Mrs. Danh realizes her daughter's hand is gone, she fearfully calls out, "Luom where are you? Stand still and wait for me. Keep on talking to me." Luom answers, "I'm here Nanny! I'm here Nanny." Mrs. Danh follows Luom's voice and finds the way back to her daughter, enveloping her in a protective hug.

The Viet Minh in Cai Nuoc always choose to attack when there is moonless night. The nights are pitch black and they cannot even see the person next to them. Yet, if they could see, then they would find their hands covered in mosquitoes. They can still hear them move through the air. The sound of their shrill buzzing is like horror music. Their hands blindly try to slap away the parasites. The holes in the ground host leeches, living on both land and water. In some areas, they mass together like thick noodles. Living conditions in this place are even harder than in the hamlet of Vinh Binh.

Isolated from the outside world, soldiers' wives must form their own market to trade their food sources. Most of their supplies come from family in the city, fish caught from the river or their small farms in the compound. Few wives have the courage to leave the compound for other market places.

The women who live in the village are Viet Minh undercover. They lure the soldiers living at the compound. Lieutenant Bay especially loves beauty, and notices the women that pass by. He visits them during the day when the Viet Minh are not willing to reveal themselves. Lieutenant Bay and his men are well known to the villagers and bring back goods that their wives need. Everything changes at nightfall, when the soldiers go out to patrol their side of the river.

Mrs. Danh becomes pregnant. When she can no longer tolerate the situation, she asks her husband to let her and their daughters return to the city. She feels brokenhearted, for her life from now on will be different without her husband beside her. On the other hand, living in the compound is brutal and the safety of the children must come first.

The idea that his wife will return to the city is a happy one for Lieutenant Bay. At once, he arranges for his family to start their trip. The boat ride back to the city is exciting for Luom, who enjoys the bouncing water as other boats pass by her. To get a better view, Luom walks to the end of the boat and sits next to a woman she believes is the owner. When Luom returns to her mother, Mrs. Danh whispers in her daughter's ear, "You are a traitor, you betray me."

"Why Nanny?"

"That woman is stealing another's husband. She slept with your father and she is carrying your father's child. Your father told her to accompany us. This is one of the reasons I want to go back to the city. Let your father have his freedom. I am too tired to be jealous. It's best for everyone."

"I didn't know, Nanny." Luom is still just a young child. She doesn't understand what her mother is going through. However, she pleases her mother by remaining at her side for the rest of the trip. When they reach the city, Mrs. Danh and the children go directly to army headquarters, asking for a new home. The army home always comes with a few beds, tables and chairs. It helps them to be more comfortable as they move in. With her pots and pans packed in their bags, in no time their new home is complete.

As soon as she is settled, Mrs. Danh sends word to her mother, asking for one of her sisters to help take care of the youngest. Ut Thom arrives excited to take her turn.

Their daily routine is empty without a husband and father. Mrs. Danh's pregnancy draws closer to the end. With the baby coming and now many months passed in separation, Mrs. Danh and the children hope to reunite soon with Lieutenant Bay.

It is the darkest night of the month, and the chirping sounds from the crickets make the dark seem even deeper. The mice run through the foliage and the sound of a struggle alerts Luom that someone's cat caught one. The dogs living in the neighborhood bark loudly. Suddenly, Ut Thom hears a rustling noise just outside. Immediately scared, she whirls to her sister's bed. While her body trembles, she breathes her words softly to wake Mrs. Danh, "Chi Tu, (sister four) wakes up! There is someone outside at the dog entrance."

Even though Mrs. Danh is at first sleepy, her mind becomes quickly alert. She picks up a big long wooden stick next to her bed and quietly goes to wait at the dog entry. The thief crawls through the dog door. Before the thief is able to stand up, Mrs. Danh strikes him as hard as she can, screaming, "Thief! Thief! Thief!"

Who knows how many words come out of her mouth? Who knows how many times she whacks him on top of his back? He raises his arms to stop the beating from her, and to surrender. "*Minh Oi!* It's me! It's me!" he pleaded.

When the second words come out of his mouth, Mrs. Danh realizes it is her husband, but remembering the other woman's child will be born as the same time as her own and how much she misses him, she beats him a few more strikes. Afterward, their love life is back to normal. Ut Thom and Luom often giggle about the drama in their love story.

A few weeks later, Mrs. Danh goes into labor. Her husband carries her to the hospital two or three miles from their home. Public transportation is unavailable in the tropical forest that is the city of Ca Mau. They must rely on walking and a bright full moon to show their way.

Luom's new brother, Diep, however, is unwilling to wait to be born at the hospital. Instead, he decides to be born beneath the romantic moonlight and closer to nature. Lieutenant Bay is forced to deliver his son on the side of the road. After the baby is born, he leaves them and run to the hospital for help.

The next morning, Lieutenant Bay brings his sister in-law, Ut Thom, to the hospital to see his wife and baby. He proudly points to the spot where the baby was born; there is still blood on the roadside.

With the new baby and Lieutenant Bay home, the sleeping arrangements changes. Luom is left with a cold, big wooden trunk as her new bed.

Shortly after, Lieutenant Bay goes back on duty, but this time to a new village. At Dam Doi, the population is a little bigger than Cai Nuoc, but it is the same as every other, a jungle swampland.

Every month as different soldiers come back to their families, they stop by and give Mrs. Danh the regular monthly income from her husband. Luom, an adventurous young girl who misses her father, asks if she can tag along with the soldiers who is visit her. Mrs. Danh agrees. Luom takes her savings and buys her father a cabbage.

The soldier asks, "What did you bring for your father?"

Luom humbly holds the cabbage closer to her chest and looks at the soldier with a smile, "A cabbage."

Her smile quickly fades, though, when the soldier says to Luom, "Just a cabbage?" Luom senses a mocking voice, but maybe she misunderstood him. In spite of this possibility, Luom feels dejected. All the money she earned running errands for people in the compound had gone to pay for this cabbage. She turns a cold shoulder to the soldier.

When the soldier and Luom reach the village, both go straight to her father. Lieutenant Bay is rather surprised by his daughter's visit, but there was no way Luom could have let her father know her plans. Yet, he is happy to see his daughter. He takes Luom around the compound and the village, introducing her to everyone. Luom feels like a princess next to her father.

Dam Doi is different from Cai Nuoc. The situation is better for the soldiers' wives. They can chitchat with outsiders. Luom is even able to go to the market with KiKi, her father's newest German shepherd (Lieutenant Bay names all his dogs KiKi).

KiKi and Luom bond at first sight. KiKi, a soldier dog, takes Luom to the market daily. It knows how to buy tobacco and fish for

Lieutenant Bay. All Lieutenant Bay has to do is write a note and KiKi carries it to the market. At each stop, the storeowners, who know KiKi, add to the bag held in its mouth. They almost never forget because if Kiki does not get what he is supposed to bring home, he stands there and stares at them. KiKi is a big dog and his gaze scares people stiff. No one wants to mess with Kiki. The villagers call Luom and KiKi, "the princess and protector."

Unfortunately, one day when KiKi, the storeowner and Luom are busy watching a fight happening next door, the storeowner forgets to put the tobacco in the can that KiKi was carrying. When Lieutenant Bay opens the lid, the can is empty and he asks, "KiKi, "KiKi, where is my tobacco?"

Listening to the angry tone of his voice and feeling hurt by a hard whack on the tail, KiKi becomes mad. He goes back to the front of the store and stands there looking fixedly at the man. From then on, neither storeowner nor KiKi forgot what they are supposed to do.

Lieutenant Bay is a busy man. He is always out with his men, days and night, leaving Luom on her own. Her father asks the woman living next door to take care of her. The woman seems to dislike Luom's presence. She is supposed to feed Luom daily. However, she hardly ever remembers. Most of the time, Luom has to find rice and cook on her own. She eats it with whatever her Father has in his place such as fish sauce or dry fish. All this time Lieutenant Bay thinks his daughter is well taken care of by his lady friend. He is unaware that Luom has been left hungry because Luom never complains.

Chapter 9
Frightened Alone in the Dark

Luom's father and Kiki are out on nightly patrol while Luom is home by herself. The sun is just beginning to set. Luom lights the beeswax candle and the mosquitoes launch themselves, buzzing their wings. She quickly lets down the mosquito net, sets the lamp on the table next to the bed and crawls in for protection.

As she lies there, she thinks of her mother. Luom misses her so much and remembers the fun she had playing with her siblings and Aunt Ut Thom. Deep in thought, Luom is suddenly disturbed by the sound of drums and tin cans. It seems like hundreds of people are beating all at once and amongst the noise, a voice shouts through the mega phone from the other side of the river. Meanwhile, Luom hears the annoyed voice of the woman next door calling her, "Luom, are you awake?"

Luom wants to answer, "Yes!" but she is voiceless. She tries to move, but her body is frozen. Her eyes are wide open. She stares at a small, creepy-crawly lizard trying to scuttle across the ceiling. The woman does not hear Luom answer. She starts calling again, "Luom, are you awake? Wake up! Bitch! You sleep so deep. If Viet Minh come in, I will let them rape you. Why don't you go home to your mother?"

The woman continues to speak with another woman on the other side of the wall about Luom and her mother, "It's not fair! I am not their slave, why do I have to watch over her. She looks exactly like her mother, ugly faces!"

43

The woman's voice is intentionally loud for Luom to hear and Luom hears all. She wants to say, "My mother is prettier than you are," but her voice is gone. Luom tries repeatedly to speak, but with no success. The woman doesn't care that Luom is still a little girl. The distance between Luom and the cold-hearted woman is only one inch, the thickness of the coconut leaf wall between them.

Luom recalls one of the stories her grandmother Ho Thiet told her, "Anyone who is cold-hearted must have cold blood and must have been a snake in their past life." Luom suddenly tires of listening to the woman, and blocks the cutting voice from her mind. Instead, she thinks about the day she will be able to go home to her mother.

Abruptly, the banging stops, and there is silence from both sides. It is as if time stands still. Luom slowly regains control of her legs and arms. To prevent anyone outside from seeing in, she blows out the beeswax candle.

Used to the darkness, Luom slowly inches her foot forward to the front window, careful not to bump into things. There is not much to bump into. The room is very small. It is just large enough to fit a full-sized bed and an end table, leaving a few paces to reach the window. There is another table, with two chairs crafted from tree branches.

Standing next to the window, Luom carefully pokes her finger into the wall, making a peep hole. The gloomy darkness fills the swampland and hints at the mystery of the myths. It leaves Luom feeling disturbed. On the other side of the river, the Viet Minh rise in single file, one by one, each person carrying a light. Some people curve to the right while some curve to the left, following their part of the river. The line twists through the darkness, looking like a long, glowing giant snake. Once more, Luom is filled with fear. Both sides begin to shoot again. She crawls back across the floor, grabs the old military blanket and slithers down to the shelter beneath the bed.

Luom finds a corner and circles her knees up to her chin, covering herself from top to bottom with the blanket, stick her mouth out of a torn hole in the blanket allowing her to breathe. She wriggles her hands to smack mosquitoes every time they land on her lips. She hopes that the Viet Minh will not come. If they do come, she hopes they will not see her. Luom pretends this is her magical blanket and that it will seal her beneath. Or, the king, her father, will march in to save her.

Next door, the cursing woman falls silent. To prevent the woman from bothering her again, Luom limits her movements. Calming herself, she starts to hum inside her head.

Luom can't count how many times the sounds of drums, tin cans and shooting start and stop throughout the night.

Finally, it ends. She waits for a long time before she crawls out of the hole in the ground.

The woman hears Luom's footsteps and without delay, comes right over to begin her criticisms. She grabs Luom's arm and squeezes tightly, her other hand pointing a finger at Luom's face, at the same time grinding her teeth, "I'll tell your father, you're spoiled badly and I'll have him send you home with your mother. I'm not your servant."

Luom almost burst out saying, "You're my servant? I have been taking care of myself." But once more, her mouth is a trap for the words inside. It bothers the woman when Luom is silent. Luom stares back at the woman, rasping her teeth and contracting her muscles to show her toughness. She pushes the woman away from her. Her action makes the woman crazy, and too upset to continue. The woman walks away. At long last, Luom's father arrives home.

The woman stops him at the front gate. In a low provocative voice that should only be used with her husband, she says, "I tried and tried to wake her up. Still, she was too deep in sleep and a girl should always be alert. Mistress Danh did not teach her appropriate manners. I worried all night about her, about you, about everyone, except myself. Please send Luom home today, now."

The woman triggers Luom's anger when she mentions that Luom was improperly taught by her mother. Luom is about to open her mouth, but the soldier standing beside her pinches her on the back and shakes his head, "No." The woman continues to tattle and complain.

She is the wife of the man second in command. Luom is too young to understand the situation. (However, when she gets home and tells her mother the story, Mrs. Danh concludes that her husband is having an affair with the woman.) Lieutenant Bay turns to his daughter and in a loving, fatherly voice says, "I'll have someone take you home today. This is no place for you."

Luom nods her head in agreement and goes inside to pack her

bag. In silence, Luom walks right out of the door without a peek at her father and without saying goodbye. Lieutenant Bay realizes he has hurt his daughter badly. However, it is true that this is a brutal place for his little girl or any little girl to be. He calls Luom back, "Wait a minute! I must find someone to take you home. You can't just go alone."

Luom answers her father with her face up to the sky and her bag dangling at her side, "I can go by myself. I know the way, and I don't need anyone."

In a normal situation, Lieutenant Bay would be upset with her answer. In this circumstance, he ignores her impolite manner. No matter what, he loves his daughter so much.

The woman points her finger at Luom again and says to Lieutenant Bay, "You see! You see what I mean. That is the bad attitude I'm talking about."

Luom grinds her teeth together, suddenly grabbing the woman's finger and bending it backward. The woman pulls away with angry outbursts, yelling at Luom, "You're a bastard! Bastard!"

The situation makes Lieutenant Bay embarrassed in front of his soldier. Fuming at the woman's words, he turns to her and with his coldest voice commands, "Hush! You go away."

The woman is frightened and quietly walks away. Lieutenant Bay squats down to the level of his daughter's eyes. "Would you wait here for me? I will come back in a moment."

He walks away with his soldier. Ten minutes go by and Lieutenant Bay reappears with the same soldier. The soldier happily volunteers to take Luom back to her mother and in return, receives a whole month off to be with his family. Lieutenant Bay hugs Luom, but there is no return of feeling in her loose arms, lack of energy or will to hug back. Without even a word to her Father, she walks away. Lieutenant Bay's heart bleeds to watch his little princess leave in this condition. He feels helpless, for he knows it does not matter what he says. His explanation will be unacceptable to her. She has his toughness and she worships the ground he walks on. Now, he has disappointed her. He hopes she is still too young to understand what is going on. Luom doesn't know the whole truth, but she still feels the hurt.

The pair walks along the side of the riverbank to the river dock. Luom's tears are beginning to drift with the flow of water on the river.

She doesn't look back to see if her father is still there. Unbidden, the soldier quietly follows her and respects her privacy.

When they reach the dock, the soldier locates a boat willing to take them back to the city. Luom finds a corner of the vessel, hugs her knees up to her chest and stays like that all the way back to the city, all day.

She gazes out of the window, deep in thought, watching the water leap. The boat arrives at the city port and they walk toward Luom's house, only a few miles away. The sun is sailing on the horizon. The soldier, a cultured and polite man, gets along easily with Luom. His voice is soft as he says to her, "If we walk fast, we can get there sooner."

Luom nods her head. The soldier wants to cheer her up and when they get close to her house, he asks her, "Would you like to race me to your house?"

Luom's face comes alive. She smiles and bobs her head happily. They take off and the soldier lets Luom take the lead. She thinks she has won when she reaches the house first.

At their destination, the sky is covered in darkness. The darkness in the city is very different from the darkness in the swampland. In the city the nighttime is soft and filled with life. Luom walks in and sees her Sister Thu Huong sitting on the front bed. As soon as Thu Huong sees Luom, she screams, "Sister Two is home! Sister Two is home!" Mrs. Danh and her other sister, Tam Choi, run out to the front room, wrap their arms around Luom and squeeze her tightly. Luom chokes up.

Chapter 10
Discovered

That night, Luom feels safe next to her mother. She no longer hears the voice of the wicked woman. Luom finds peace and sleeps through the night, with no disruptions from guns, drums, tin cans or mega phones.

A short while later, Ut Thom comes back to replace Tam Choi in her duties. Tam Choi has to go back to her parents and prepare to get married. Tam Choi is a very quiet and soft-spoken person. She never argues with anyone. She accepts the marriage without a fight.

Ut Thom and Luom are only a few years different in age and are happy to stay together. Both are more like best friends than aunt and niece.

They come up with an idea to earn some money. Luom and Ut Thom go door to door grooming people's heads by picking out the grey hair and lice. The business does well but the pay is low, because they allow the customers to set the price. Even so, Luom is happy with her activity.

Although usually busy working, Luom keeps her eyes on her mother. Mrs. Danh has been sneaking out of the back door every day, her hand always clutching a bowl of cooked rice. Luom's suspects her mother is feeding someone with their food, but who? The question stays in her mind and one day she decides to follow. Mrs. Danh is unaware that her clever daughter has been watching her every move. Unintentionally, she leads Luom right into the secret place that she has been visiting.

Two women hide in the tall bamboo grass. Luom recognizes one as her mother, and the other is Mrs. Phuc, their neighbor. Mrs. Phuc has been whining in self-pity, waiting for Mrs. Danh to arrive. The tall grasses also swallow Luom's small body and conceal her until she reaches the front door. She freely walks in, much to their surprise. Mrs. Phuc complains to Mrs. Danh, "Why did you bring your daughter here?"

Luom is displeased with Mrs. Phuc's attitude toward her mother. She quickly responds, "Nanny didn't bring me here. I heard your moaning from outside the field. Why are you ungrateful to my Nanny? She has been feeding you."

Mrs. Phuc knows she has triggered Luom's defensiveness, and she didn't want to give this little girl a reason to be furious. Luom is known as the girl no one can push over. In her misery, Mrs. Phuc expresses her pain, "My husband has been beating me every day."

While telling this to Luom, she pulls her hair back to show her bruises. Luom's eyes open wide in shock. She pulls herself back a few steps in fear. She has never seen anything like this before. Beside Mrs. Phuc's black eyes, there are dark patches left on the surface of old and new bruised skin. Luom is terrified.

After a few moments, Luom recovers herself and asks Mrs. Phuc, "What did you do so wrong? Whatever you have done, he has no right to treat you this way."

Sobbing, Mrs. Phuc answers, "I don't know what I have done other than cook and wait for him to come home every day for lunch. While he eats, he criticizes me and after that, he gives me a good beating. He took me to bed, petted me just like a little baby and demanded me to beg him for forgiveness. After my begging, we had sex."

Mrs. Danh complains to Mrs. Phuc, "You could have left out the end part. My daughter is still a young child."

Mrs. Phuc says, "Troi dat oi (Heaven and Earth) she should know this. It is important for her future."

Mrs. Danh replies, "But not to be told by you."

Fortunately, for Mrs. Danh, Luom understands everything except the sex part. No matter how smart she thinks she is, Luom is still in the dark about the birds and the bees. Luom turns to her mother and says, "Don't you worry Nanny, no one will beat me this way. And don't you and father arrange my marriage." Mrs. Danh takes her hand and swings at her daughter's head as hard as she can.

"That hurt!" Luom screams.

Mrs. Danh says, "You are only six years old and you are telling me not to arrange your marriage? What are you? A daughter of Te Thien Dai Thanh, the monkey King?"[1]

Rubbing her head, Luom thrusts out her lips. "I'm six and a half years old! I am not going to let this happen to me when I grow up. You and everyone else have been telling me that you picked me from outside the road, because I was unwanted. Therefore, I'm not your real daughter."

Mrs. Danh is shocked at Luom's words, but she realizes it is not Luom's fault. Her daughter has been hearing those words since she was born. How would anyone expect Luom to know differently?

Luom walks away and finds her aunt. Ut Thom asks, "Where have you been? I have been looking for you."

Still anxious, Luom tells her aunt about the episode. Ut Thom says, "I'm not going to get married when I grow up. It's too much work. Are you going to get married later? Would you give me one of your children?" (Little did Luom know that Ut Thom never would marry, but years later would raise Luom's first-born child.)

Luom looks at her aunt, "If the husband is like that, no thank you. I am going to find my own husband. No one will arrange my marriage."

"Tough girl, did you tell your father yet?"

Luom acts smugly, "He knows."

Ut Thom chuckles, "Aren't you afraid of your father?"

"No,"

As they continue speaking about life, Mrs. Danh walks in, and, overhearing, asks, "You both think you are smarter than me?"

For some reason, both are afraid of Mrs. Danh. At the same time they answer, "No Nanny! No Chi Tu!"

They do not want her to cry or get upset. However, Mrs. Danh

---

1   This is about a Chinese myth. Te Thien Dai Thanh was a monkey, but he looked human and was said to be born from a big rock. Often people used this expression to make a point with their children when they misbehave.)

is a strong woman and Luom has never seen her mother cry.

August is the monsoon season. Vietnamese people believe the rains are tears from "Ngu Lang Chuc Nu."[2]

Heavy showers fall every day without stopping. There is nothing to do, except keep each other company. Day after day, Luom stares out of the window, watching the rainfall. The river's current grows rapidly stronger. Luom hopes to see someone other than the neighbor walking by or imagines that by some magic, her father will come home. Finally, her wish is granted. A man wearing a raincoat, his face covered, walks with a dog beside him. They walk toward the house and Luom nervously gets off the chair. She runs out to the patio, bends her knees, claps her hands on top of them and screams, "Nanny, someone is coming!"

Mrs. Danh runs out and looks on as the man gets closer and closer. He looks like Lieutenant Bay. Luom moves restlessly back and forth. The man walks onto the patio, removes his coconut hat and Luom immediately screams out, "Father! Lieutenant Bay!"

Lieutenant Bay has adopted the French custom. Right away, he kisses his wife. She is impressed with his attention. Women are very attracted to his romantic ways and, with all the temptations; Lieutenant Bay has difficulty staying faithful to his wife.

Everyone is happy now that Lieutenant Bay is home. Mrs. Danh is very shy and does not know how to express her love to her husband other than, "Good, now you can fix the leaks in the roof. Luom has been running around to put buckets to catch the dripping water." As both walk in the house, she says to her husband, "I will cook rice and dry fish. You must be hungry?"

"Luom run to the store. Buy your father some Tamarind so he can eat it with his dry fish."

Luom puts on her father's raincoat and his coconut hat. Both are too big for her body. Though it looks like no one is inside the raincoat, KiKi recognizes Luom; it runs right over and licks her all over her face. Luom likes KiKi, but she dislikes the licking. Luom makes an ugly face and tries to get away. The more she tries to get away, the more KiKi

---

2 There is a fairy tale that two Angels from heaven fall in love, but they are forbidden to be together by both side's parents. The parents separated them and every year they try to reunite. Their tears become our rain.

licks.

KiKi follows Luom to the store. After they come back, the family has dinner together. After, Ut Thom whispers in Luom's ear, "Stay out here. Let your mother and your father have their time together."

That night, the coconut thatched bungalow is filled with joy. Luom sits next to her father, waiting for him to tell stories. Ut Thom is very respectful of her brother in-law. She must live in this family and grow up with some discipline just as Luom has. She is delighted with her sister's happiness.

Lieutenant Bay goes to work each morning and comes home at night. Their life seems steady and is never dull with him around. Some afternoons, he waits for the low tide, and rain or shine goes down to the Kinh 16 (river 16). He sticks his hand in mud holes to pull up eels. He throws them up on the riverbank for Ut Thom and Luom to pick up. KiKi runs around barking and snatching the eels, then drops them in a bucket. Thu Huong is only two and a half years old and even she has as much fun as everyone else chasing after the eels. Luom's brother Diep wiggles in Mrs. Danh's arms and does not miss any excitement.

Lieutenant Bay is a man who likes to gain knowledge. He is always learning new things. He picks up guitar. At night after dinner, he plays Vietnamese folk music. The guitar fascinates Luom, who sits beside her father and sings along with him. Life is as stable as it can be.

Chapter 11
Back to Hometown

Their peaceful life ends when Lieutenant Bay comes home to tell his wife to pack up all their belongings. He has been discharged from the military. They are to go back to their hometown.

Before the trip begins, Lieutenant Bay calls Luom over to him. He warns her, "This is a very difficult time for me. I want you to zip your lips, don't complain and no giving orders to everyone on this journey home. Do you understand?"

Luom stands straight as a soldier and salutes her father. "Yes sir, Lieutenant Bay!" Thu Huong sees Luom do this and she comes to stand right next to Luom, copying her movements. Their hilarious act squeezes a chuckle out of their father. Lieutenant Bay says to his daughters, "From now on, I am just Mr. Bay. To you two, I am your father. Agreed?"

Luom and Thu Huong say in unison, "Yes, sir! I mean—yes father."

Early on the third morning, the wagon man shows up to carry the trunk full of their belongings to the bus station. There is no soldier to accompany them. They all walk next to the wagon quietly. KiKi is a smart dog and, sensing problems, silently trots beside Luom.

Yesterday, Mr. Bay was Lieutenant Bay and now, in just a short time, he is nobody. Mr. Bay's life has never been predictable. He considers this new trial easy in comparison. He can go back to his parents and start a new life. It will be fine, he assures himself. At least from now on, he will be home every night with his wife and children.

It not difficult to find the bus to his hometown. There is only one road to the south and there are few other busses at the station.

As the bus wheels begins to roll, Mr. Bay's mind begins to spin as well. There are many questions to consider such as what he is going doing next. His life before he joined the army still haunts him. He never wants to face it again. Yet, he realizes that it was many years ago and things have changed. The country has altered many ways of life. There is no more Dien Chu (Title of rice paddies own.) or slavery in this generation. His life is his own. He does not have to answer to anyone. He will make it somehow.

The atmosphere within the bus is celebratory with sounds of loud voices and laughter from the people. It is like one big party. Unfortunately, Mr. Bay and his family are not there to celebrate. Instead, they are all silent. It is difficult for Luom to sit next to her father. Every time she starts to ask a question, he turns to her with a sharp glance and Luom knows right then to shut her mouth before she gets in trouble. KiKi patiently lies on the bus floor, allowing Luom to pet it and busy herself.

The bus reaches their destination after dropping Ut Thom off at her house. They continue a short distance and get off the bus by the river's edge near where Mr. Bay's parents live. Mr. Bay yells out to his brothers, "Ut or Khanh! Come on over to pick us up."

From the other side of the river, family members hear the shout, and run out to see who has called. When they recognize Mr. Bay, smiles light their faces as they holler back, "Hey Bay! About time you come home."

Mrs. Ho Thiet especially misses her son. He is her symbol of hope in life and he is a provider for everyone. No matter how far Mr. Bay travels, he always takes good care of his parents and siblings. Mrs. Ho Thiet shouts, "I'm going into the kitchen to cook your favorite dish."

Mr. Ngoc waves his hand to welcome his son. Meanwhile, Ut Mot, Mr. Bay's younger brother, paddles over in a canoe. It takes several trips for the family and their belongings to cross the river.

The dinner table is like a big party that afternoon. Family

members are eager to ask Mr. Bay questions. After so many years, they are finally reunited as a family. As for Mrs. Danh, she must wait until the following day to see her relatives.

At dawn, Mr. Bay helps his wife dress up the children. They set off to Mrs. Danh's parents to join them for breakfast. Ut Thom has been watching the road to catch the first glimpse of their shadow. When she sees them in the distance, Ut Thom yells out to her parents, "Mother and Father! They are coming!"

Mr. Duong complains to his daughter, "Girls shouldn't shout like that. You can walk in to tell us."

Ut Thom answers, "I'm just excited father."

Mr. Duong replies, "But you just parted with them yesterday."

"Yes, but I like to play with Luom."

Mrs. Duong says to Mr. Duong, "You just have to learn to let the children be themselves."

It is cheerful for all when the family reunites with their son and daughter. Mr. Bay is a generous man and respected by both sides of the family. When he mentions he needs help to build a new home for his wife and children, all are happy to volunteer.

The next morning before the sun rises Mrs. Danh's siblings show up at Mrs. Ho Thiet's residence to help Mr. Bay sketch the plan for the new house and find the materials for construction. First, they journey deep into the jungle and chop big trees for the main structure. Next, Mr. Bay finds coconut leaves for the roof and uses rice straw mixed with riverbed mud for the walls. When the walls dry, the seashells become visible and add a decorative touch to the outside and inside of the house. For the floor, they pound down clay until it is tightly packed. As soon as the floor is dry, they sprinkle water over the ground and smooth it with their hands until it becomes even and glossy.

Luom is thrilled with this big home. For the first time in her life, she can run inside and outside freely. She feels relaxed knowing this is her parents' home and no longer a military compound. Mr. Bay turns the back of the house into a workshop where he can manufacture cement pots. The pots will be use to store fish, rice and rainwater or other essentials.

The villagers usually dig ponds in their backyards to store rainwater, but Mr. Bay remembers how his second daughter Thu

Huong almost died from drowning in a pond. He says a pond is out of the question. Mr. Bay lines the pots alongside the house to show off his work, while also using them to catch rainwater. The villagers, seeing his clever demonstration, come from near and far to buy the pots. They trade with their harvested rice, pig, money, gold, and anything they can. Soon Mr. Bay is well known for his craft.

Both sides of the family have plenty of work from Mr. Bay. Regardless of his busy schedule, Mr. Bay always sets aside time to spend with his daughter out in the rice paddies, picking snails. At the first rainfall, the snails come close to the surface, and Mr. Bay and Luom dig them out of the ground with knives. The snails are fat and have a rich taste. Yet, when the rain falls for more than a few weeks, the rice paddies fill with water and the snails float on top. It is easy to pick them then, but the meat is tough and tasteless.

Besides having fun with her father, Luom often asks to accompany her aunts out in the rice paddies. Unluckily for Luom, she is unaware when a leech begins to suck on her ankle. When she realizes, her heart beats fast from fear. She screams loudly, bringing both of her aunts to the rescue. One tries to hold her leg while the other attempts to rub it off with a bundle of grass. By the time they are able to control her flailing, the leech has long gone, having sucked its fill.

Mr. Bay is an active man. He is always working. The job he enjoys the most is fishing, usually with Luom tagging along close beside him. In Viet Nam, food sources from the land are abundant. All they have to do is put the fishing line into the water and eventually they have enough fish to take home. Mr. Bay's fishing rod dips down and he catches a fish. For Luom, this seems impossible as she peers into the water, the tall cattails grasses swaying above her head. Luom bounces up and down like a rabbit. Her behavior strikes Mr. Bay as funny and he laughs. He takes her stick and casts for her. Immediately, she catches a fish. Luom runs around, screaming at the top of her lungs. Mr. Bay smiles again at his daughter's joy.

Fish fill the basket. Father and daughter head home. On the way back, Luom spots a water lily pond. She turns around and asks Bay, "Father, would you please help me pick some water lilies?"

"You want to have that for tonight's meal?"

"Yes! Also, I want to sell some at the market tomorrow."

"No one will buy that."

"Why Father?"

"Everyone picks their own water lilies, it's free. Why would they want to pay?"

"What if they don't want to go pick?"

"Remember this, I don't want you have to live farmer life style. Just grow up and go to school."

"Just this time Father."

Even Mr. Bay knows that no one will buy his daughter's water lilies. But he wants to do something for her anyway. He sinks his body into the pond and pulls up the whole plant of water lilies. Only ten minutes later, he has a bundle of water lilies for Luom.

When Luom and her father get home, Luom goes straight to cut up her lilies. She puts them into a small bundle and prepares to sell them in the morning at the market.

At 5am, Luom hears her father's footsteps and gets up. They both get ready and head to the dock and row the boat down river. Mr. Bay tells his daughter, "Any time you want to go home, just say so." Luom nods and says, "I'm going to make a lot of money today!"

When they reach the market, Luom find a spot to display her water lilies. People walk by, but none of them are interested enough to buy any. Although he is busy talking to people, Mr. Bay keep his eyes on his daughter. He saw her face wondering why people don't buy her water lilies. He steps over and whispering into her ear, "Asks them."

"How, Father?"

"Like this. Moi ba mua bong sung cua con." (Mrs. Buy my water lily.")

She asks many, but they all shake their heads, No. Finally Mr. Bay says to his daughter, "Let's go home. We can't sell them all, what will we have for our dinner tonight?"

Luom quickly gets up and carries all her water lilies in their bundle. She walks off with her father. She promises herself that she will have to listen to her father from now on.

When they get home, Mrs. Danh asks, "Did you sell any water lilies?"

Mr. Bay robs the answer from Luom, "She wanted to sell them all, but I wanted them for tonight supper."

Mrs. Danh says to her husband, "Then you must have a craving for Bun Nuoc Leo?" (The famous stinky soup, cooked with fermented fishes, might smell unpleasant, but is a favorite for some Vietnamese families.)

"You have read my mind. I had that thought all morning, but I was afraid Luom would not agree with me."

Innocently, Luom says to her father, "Father, you could have just told me."

Mr. Bay kisses his wife and says, "I can't wait for my specialty." Mr. Bay enjoys his Bun Nuoc Leo with his wife and children that night.

Chapter 12
School

In the village, radios and record players begin to emerge in everyday households. Famous singers and stories are heard on the radio. Luom gets an idea from one of the stories and begins to practice sword fighting. This way, she thinks, she will be able to go anywhere she wants and no longer be scared. One of her fears was of walking to school. She makes Thu Huong and some of her cousins' battle with her regularly in preparation.

Three miles lie between Luom's house and school. There are two ways to get there. Luom can have one of her aunts or uncles canoe her across the river, or she can walk by country road. Only one or two cars go by every hour on that road. She is terrified to think she will have to walk by herself. There are large trees and only a few houses between home and school. The lonely surroundings discourage her.

On the other hand, if she takes the jungle trail, she doesn't have to rely on anyone to row her across the river. Luom likes to be independent. Yet, if she walks through the jungle, both sides of the trail have more trees and bushes than the other way. Luom picks the jungle way. At least this way she won't have to worry about being hit by a car. The distance of both ways is the same.

Luom plans her trek through the jungle for a whole week and considers what will make her feel more secure. At last, she stumbles upon an idea, "Aha! I will make myself a wooden sword."

When Mrs. Danh sees her daughter outside the yard chopping a tree branch, she asks her, "What are you doing with that, daughter?" "This is for my protection."

Mrs. Danh starts to giggle, "Protection from what?"

Luom continues to chop the tree branch as she answers her mother, "From the monster, Nanny."

Mrs. Danh warns her daughter, "Careful, don't chop your hand off."

Just as the words leave Mrs. Danh's lips, Luom screams. Her high-pitched voice frightens her mother. Luom grasps her hand to her chest; her arm is drenched in blood. Everyone nearby runs over. Luom's little finger is severed just below the nail.

Mr. Bay cradles his daughter and carries her inside. He soaks her finger with a piece of wet tobacco to stop the bleeding and wraps it in a tight cloth. There is no doctor in the village and the family must settle for what is within their means. Unfortunately, the next day Luom comes down with a fever. Mr. Bay tells his wife, "It is wise to take her to a doctor."

Mrs. Danh quickly agrees with her husband, "Let's go."

Both leave with Luom and paddle across the river. They sit on the side of the road, waiting for the bus to come. It takes nearly an hour before it finally shows up. The road to Bac Lieu is no picnic and they are jolted up and down the whole way. However the discomfort is replaced with worry when halfway there they notice small blotches of red appearing on Luom's body.

Putting a hand to her forehead, they realize Luom's fever is getting higher. At last, they reach the hospital where their daughter is finally in the good hands of the doctor. Husband and wife now feel less anxious but they must remain in the hospital.

A few days later, the doctor says to Luom's parents, "She should be well enough to leave here tomorrow."

Mr. Bay is bothered, "But those red dots..."

The doctor replies, "I really don't know what to make of those red blemishes. I have never seen anything like this before, but she is going to be fine."

Mr. Bay has to take his daughter back without a diagnosis. Soon they arrive home. Mr. Bay and Mrs. Danh prepare an in home remedy treatment. Luom stands on the bed and Mrs. Danh begins to burn wet coconut leaves. The smoke rises up Luom's body to help cure the itchiness from the red blemishes. Luom has to jump around on the bed to prevent getting burned. The next morning, the red dots on Luom's body begin to fade away.

To show his love for his daughter, Mr. Bay finishes the wooden sword to protect her against monsters on her way to school.

After Mr. Bay had carved the wooden sword, Mrs. Ho Thiet came right over to teach her granddaughter some sword fighting skills. Mr. Bay tells his mother, "Mother, you don't need to teach her all that."

Mrs. Ho Thiet looks at her son. "Let me have some fun with my granddaughter. Hush, go away."

"Luom's mind must have some of your influence."

"Well, she has my blood."

Mr. Bay wants his daughter to be a soft little girl, but his mother insists she be tough like her. Mr. Bay, not wanting to disrespect his mother, walks away.

On the first day of school, Mr. Bay asks Luom, "Would you like me to take you to school?"

Luom answers her father, "I am going to be fine, father. I have my sword."

Mr. Bay is uneasy about his daughter's way of thinking. It is unnatural for her to be thinking this way. He thinks the war must be affecting her badly. Luom often has nightmares. However, he decides to let her mind lead her. Mrs. Danh asks Luom, "Are you dressed yet?"

"Yes Nanny! I am ready."

Mr. Bay calls to her, "Then come out here! Let us take a look at the big girl on her first day of school."

Luom walks out to stand in front of her parents, shy in the new outfit that her Uncle Bay Thoi has made for her. Her father admires her. "You look very pretty."

Luom glances sideways at her father, "Father, don't tease me."

"No," Mrs. Danh says, "your father is right. You are a pretty little girl. Now, this is your lunch and your ferry money. Go on to school."

As Luom begins to walk, her mind is alert to the monsters that she will face on the trail to school. Self-confident, she knows she will win the battle if any monster jumps out from the bushes; she has been practicing with her sword, the way her grandmother taught her. Luom imagines herself as a powerful princess. She leaps, beats at the bushes, her sword dancing to push the beast out in the open.

However, there are no beasts, only birds and frogs. Later, she sees a fox. Villagers travel from the opposite side of the trail and Luom spots them from far away. She continues to play out her act, bowing momentarily to pay her respect.

At the end of the trail, she pays Ong Lai Do, the canoe man, to cross the river. The canoe lands at her Uncle Ba Vit's port, which lies in back of his house.

Luom begins school late for her age. Many children her age are already in the second grade and know how to read. Luom does not even know what the alphabet is. She sits in the classroom, feeling rather dumb. Yet she knows she is not stupid, she just has to learn faster. School is fun for her, too, with half of the classroom full of her cousins, and all of the other students her same age. Encouraging herself, she thinks, "I will be fine. I will catch up." Luom and her cousins' play together, eat together and go to school together.

One day after school, Luom and her cousin, her Uncle Ba Vit's daughter Bia, eat rice together. Bia says something to Luom, and Luom answers back smartly. Bia quickly becomes upset. While Luom holds up her cracked rice bowl to eat, her cousin places her hand beneath it and shoves upward. The bowl smashes into Luom's chin. The cracked rice bowl cuts Luom's chin badly. However, Ba Vit does not believe in punishing his children. He comes over to show his love and care for Luom, but leaves Bia alone.

After lunch, they all head to their grandmother's house to play and do their homework. Unfortunately, things do not go too smoothly there either. In the middle of doing math, Luom again says something clever. Her cousin Thanh To takes her little chalkboard and brings it down on Luom's head. It goes down to her eyes and gives her another scar on the left eyebrow. It is difficult for Luom who knows what she is talking about. The others might have been in school before her, but Luom is older and she feels she is smarter than they are.

The second incident with her other cousin causes Luom to reconsider her words. From now on, she decides, it is best not to express her knowledge to anyone else. Right or wrong, she should keep it to herself.

Luom gets bored. With nothing to do but sit around and talk, she no longer finds the company of her cousins desirable. Luom overhears someone mention a woman named Ba Tam Sen who lives across the road. She has just had a baby, now a few weeks old. The mother walks around without clothing and because of that, she never walks outside to see if someone enters her yard. A tamarind tree in full bloom grows in the yard. Although the flowers and leaves are very sour, they are good to munch on in the afternoon. Yet no one dares to trespass. Luom asks her cousins to show her the way; they say to each other, "She can't even cross the road without someone to hold her hand. How is she supposed to get there?"

Another cousin complains, "She is going to eat all the flowers and leaves. There will be nothing left for us."

The other one says, "Don't worry so much, she won't be able to."

Luom soon proves them wrong. She studies the fence, looking to find a way in. Every day for a week, she neglects to play with her cousins. Some ask where she is. One answers, "She thinks she can get a snack over there. Let her dream, who is going to take her across the road other than us? She is so scared of the caterpillars, she won't be able to eat the leaves."

They underestimate Luom, who starts crossing the road herself and secretly lies in wait in front of the fence. One afternoon, Luom spots an opportunity. The woman goes to sleep. In a flash, Luom climbs over the fence carefully, leaps lightly past the front door of the house and heads to the tree. Without any problems, she clambers up, and finds a spot where she can lean on to rest her back on a larger branch. She puts her two legs out, one on each branch for support. Now nicely situated, Luom treats herself to a yummy snack. In that moment, she looks like a happy monkey. After three visits, the tree starts to show signs of the invasion, and Luom's cousin tips off the woman. Soon, Ba Tam Sen has no doubt of her quiet invader.

On an afternoon like any other, Luom sits enjoying her snacks in her monkey-like position. Suddenly, she hears footsteps coming closer and closer. Nervous, she realizes this is her last chance to nibble.

In a hurry, with one hand Luom grabs a handful of leaves and puts them into her mouth, with the other hand she tosses in the salt. Luom chews them quickly together. Suddenly, she feels a squishy pop inside her mouth. Her eyes widen as she realizes she has bitten into a caterpillar. Her heart races dreadfully, her hands shake, and losing her balance, she falls off the tree to land hard on her back. While she is suffering from the pain, Luom hears a voice above her head, "You must be hurting badly? I told all of you to leave this tree alone. When there are fruits, I'll give you some. Let the tree have a chance to produce."

Ba Tam Sen is unfamiliar with the taste of the flowers and leaves of tamarind tree. To Luom, it tastes better than the fruit. Luom opens her eyes and looks up. Ba Tam Sen stands naked above her head. Luom has never seen a nude body before other than the unclothed children running around during the rainy season. Anxiously, Luom dashes off. On the other side of the fence, all her cousins crouch with their hands covering their mouths, giggling. Luom passes by them and walks away. She will not soon forget that painfully embarrassing moment. Never again does she return to the tree.

Although Luom remains upset, the memory of the tree is fresh in her mind. She quickly finds a different way to amuse herself. She begins to explore her grandmother's property. Mrs. Duong has many things growing, but none of her trees provides edible flowers or leaves. Yet, Luom soon discovers the guava fruits. At just few months old, they are sour and crunchy, making for a great snack. For something to eat with them Luom takes a net, catches all of her grandmother's newborn snakefish heads in the pond, and enters the kitchen to cook herself a fantastic lunch.

One of the cousins tells Mrs. Duong, "Grandmother, Luom ate all of your fruits and your newborn fishes."

Mrs. Duong smiles and replies, "Oh, it's fine; besides, the fishes would go away if she didn't eat them, and the fruits will come back again. There is no need to be alarmed."

None of the grandchildren dare to follow Luom's example. Mrs. Duong would have thrown a fit. For some reason, Luom's newfound activity does not seem to matter to her.

Sometimes, Luom and her father sneak into the chicken barn. At every nest, they take one egg and poke a tiny hole into it, then suck it dry and place it back into the nest. When it is time for the eggs to hatch, every nest has one empty egg. Mrs. Duong merely smiles and shakes her head, saying to Luom, "Your father taught you another trick?"

Mrs. Duong always takes notice of Luom and sees that she doesn't like to sit still. To keep her busy, she hands Luom a fishing pole and tells her, "Go down to the river and catch yourself dinner." Luom does as her grandmother says.

The river water flows steadily from the ocean, bringing in all varieties of fish. Luom happens to catch a baby shark. Her cousins yell out, "Luom caught a shark! Luom caught a shark!" Everyone nearby runs over to admire her. She feels rather happy with all the attention.

Luom loves to listen her grandfather play music. Sometimes Luom asks permission from her parents to stays overnight at Mrs. Duong's house. At one o'clock in the morning, Luom and her aunt are wakened by her grandfather, Mr. Duong, saying, "Luom and Ut Thom! Wake up and sing for me."

Neither dares to complain when Mr. Duong disturbs their sleep. They jump out of bed and head to the front of the house. Mr. Duong starts to play music long before he awakens them. He enjoys Vietnamese folk music like his son-in-law Mr. Bay does. However, the instrument he plays is quite different. The Don Co has only two strings. Sometimes, the music is sad to Luom while at other times it makes her feel like she is lost in a cloud, especially when she is half asleep. Into this cloud flits the scent of the freshly harvested rice, from Mrs. Duong's kitchen, making it impossible for Luom not to wake up, when the scent reaches her nose.

At two o'clock in the morning, everyone heads out to the rice paddies to work. By ten o'clock, before the heat of the sun rises, they all have to return home.

Chapter 13
The Uninvited

Rice farming and ceramics are not enough to tie Mr. Bay down. Life seems dull to him. Often, he goes off at nights without telling his family of his whereabouts. One night, after Mrs. Danh had just climbed into her bed, a knock comes at the door. Mrs. Danh calls out, "Who is it?"

The voice from outside responds, "We're friends of Mr. Bay and we are visiting him. Open the door."

Inside Mrs. Danh yells out, "My husband is out."

A different voice demands, "We recommend you open the door. We just want to talk."

Mrs. Danh repeats, "I told you my husband is out."

The other side again pressures. "Then you have nothing to worry. If we find he is gone, we will leave. Open the door now. We will not go away until you open it."

Mrs. Danh thinks it is safe to open the door. If they meant any harm, they would have already burst into the house. After all, her house is a coconut hut, and the door is just tied to a wooden stick. Slowly, Mrs. Danh unknots the rope to let them in. The group of three men follows Mrs. Danh into and around the house. When they reach the bedroom, the men take their flashlights and shine it on the bed. Luom recognizes the trousers and shirts on the men as similar to the ones her father wears. One of the men turns to Mrs. Danh. "Where is your husband?"

Mrs. Danh looks at him. "He hasn't been home for weeks."

"When will he be home?"

"I don't really know."

Meanwhile, next door, Mrs. Ho Thiet hears the commotion and she dashes over to see what is going on. Mrs. Ho Thiet reaches the bedroom, and after assessing the situation, asks them, "Why are you looking for my son?"

"We are his friends, and we want to talk to him."

Mrs. Ho Thiet quickly becomes angry. "If you are his friends, you wouldn't come here in the middle of the night, demanding to look all over his house!"

She continues forcefully, "Go away! Leave my daughter in-law and my grandchildren alone."

Following her words, she takes the broomstick and hits one of the men in the rear. She sweeps at the floor with hard strokes, moving toward them.

"Out! Out!"

One of the men says, "Old woman! You have the guts to strike us?"

Mrs. Ho Thiet responds, "You want me to be polite? Then come in the daytime—with manners!"

The men, realizing they are getting nowhere with Mrs. Ho Thiet, decide to leave. Mrs. Danh goes down to the kitchen, lights the stove and heats the water to make her mother in-law a cup of tea with a bit of brown sugar. Mrs. Ho Thiet enjoys the midnight snack. In a little while, again comes a knock on the door. Thinking that the men are back for more questions, she asks, "What is it now?"

A voice from other side says, "Let us in."

Mrs. Ho Thiet pushes her daughter in-law out of the way and is about to scream out as she opens the door when she suddenly realizes this is a different group. In an ill-mannered tone, she asks them, "Who are you people? Why are so many people looking for my son?"

One of them responds, "Who else is looking for him? We are his friends."

Rudely, Mrs. Ho Thiet says, "Everybody is his friend. Go away and come back when he is here." Unfortunately, her unkind manner does not deter them. These men too make their way into the house, forcing Mrs. Danh to shine the bedroom oil lamp over the childrens' faces while they are peacefully sleeping. All except Luom, she was wide-awake from the beginning.

Displeased with their fruitless effort, the second group of men leave Mrs. Danh's house. Later in life, Luom realizes the first group was the South Viet Nam government and the second group was the Viet Cong.[3] With the disruptions past, silence returns to the darkness of the night. Mrs. Ho Thiet goes back to her cup of tea. While she sips the tea slowly, suddenly a machine gun sounds in the distance, "Tach, tach, tach...."

Mrs. Ho Thiet asks her daughter in-law, "Danh, did you hear that?"

"Yes! Mother, I heard them too."

"We're too far from the Army post, so you don't have to worry. But I'm going to sleep here tonight with all of you."

"What about father? You don't want to go back over there with him?"

"He will be fine because he has others around him. I feel uncomfortable leaving you with all the children."

In the meantime, Luom softly comes to sit in between her grandmother and her mother. Mrs. Danh asks Luom, "Why aren't you as sleep?"

Luom answer, "How could I sleep with all this going on, Nanny?"

Looking at her mother in-law, Mrs. Danh asks for permission, "Mother, I would like to go back with my other children."

"Go, Luom will be here with me."

Before sunrise, Mrs. Ho Thiet readies herself to walk to town. Luom has been waiting to go with her Grandmother. Mrs. Danh tells Luom, "Don't go."

"It is going to be fine. Don't worry." Mrs. Ho Thiet smiles at Luom.

Mrs. Ho Thiet and Luom walk off to the river, both hop in the canoe and Mrs. Ho Thiet paddles her canoe downstream. 30 minutes

---

3   Viet Cong were supported and trained by the communist North Viet Nam to oppose the French. Japanese and American.

later, they land the canoe at Ba Vit's dock behind his house. Mrs. Ho Thiet ties the rope and she and Luom climb the ladder and enter through the back. In the front of the house, they find Mrs. Duong is there as well. People are frantically scurrying about, shouting at one another. One man is dead in the front yard at Ba Vit's house and another body has been discovered in someone's bathroom.

Mrs. Ho Thiet rushes into the crowd of people searching for the bodies. Luom, not wanting to lose sight of her grandmother, runs after her. Luom makes her way through a small circle of people to the source of the gathering. A man lies on the ground; curled into a protective position, loose black clothing identifying him as one of the Viet Cong. He is dead. Luom stares at him in horror and her face pales. Seeing she is about to collapse, Mrs. Duong runs for a wet cloth to put on Luom's face, at the same time asking Mrs. Ho Thiet, "Would you take her home?"

Mrs. Ho Thiet quickly agrees. About time they reach home, Mr. Bay is waiting for them at the front door after a month's disappearance and accompanied by the local army soldiers. Turning to his mother, he asks, "Mother, why did you take Luom into town while all this was going on?"

Ignoring the question, Mrs. Ho Thiet replies, "She is fine. Where have you been?"

"Never mind where I was, I will explain it to you later, mother. My wife and my children have to leave right now."

"Right now? In this moment?"

"Yes, immediately."

Mr. Ngoc and his family are surprised by Mr. Bay's quick decision. Yet, they know Mr. Bay's method. He warns no one in advance.

He continues, "Father, Mother, you must sell all the land and our houses with it."

"What do you want us to do with no home?" Mrs. Ho Thiet asks.

"For the time being, just pack your bags and take the bus to Ho Phong. Go to the police station, I will be waiting for you there. Sell the land and houses later."

Mrs. Danh swiftly packs what belongings she can. They cross

the river and hop in Mr. Bay's new Jeep, destined for a new home. The trip is brief, only about fifteen miles from their old house. Mr. Bay has built a new home for his family. The front of the house faces the road. Just across the road are his compound and the local police station, including a jail. Mr. Bay, as the new Chief of Police, conducts all of the business related to the public.

A lagoon wraps around back of the house and one side of Mr. Bay's house. Next to Mr. Bay's, there is a little bungalow for people in the village to rest in the hot afternoon or rain while waiting for Mr. Bay's office to open. Adjacent to the bungalow is a private school. The lagoon then extends a half mile from the borders of the school to Mrs. Ho Thiet and Mr. Bay's younger brother Ut Mot's new home. Ba Di Nam, Mr. Bay's aunt, has a home beside theirs. Mr. Bay has managed to build all this in the month he was absent from home.

Mr. Ngoc will be living with Mr. Bay's family. Mr. Bay's face shines with love for his father. To make him happier, he creates a cement flower box for Mr. Ngoc to plant a garden along the fence in the front yard.

A watchtower stands tall in the middle of the triangular compound to help the Police Chief and his men see far into the distance. At each of the three corners, there is a low watch post meant to help detect enemies trying to crawl in along the ground. Four single beds lie in each of the watch post, for the four men inside. They take turns, two on guard and two asleep. Along the three walls of the compound, Mr. Bay erects living quarters for the families all of his men. One room for each families and one is for Mr. Bay' family to sleep in; but for others, this single room is the only home they have.

To enter the compound, a person must cross ten L-shaped bridges perched atop sturdy wooden spares, zigzagging to their destination. During high tide, however, they lie underneath the water, invisible, until rising into view again at low tide. The River is swimming with plenty of fish for everyone.

Barbed wires wrap like a spider's web around the compound. Within the entanglements lie explosives, the nail beds set beneath the ground's surface. The Police Chief has placed them carefully.

Understanding the danger they pose, Police Chief Bay warns his daughter, "Luom, listen to me carefully. It is dangerous around the compound." He points and continues, "Look, I had to put explosives in those barbed wires. Make sure you stay away."

Luom nods her head, "Yes father."

Nevertheless, the new surroundings fascinate Luom. She enjoys the adventure while most other children would have rested in the afternoon. For some reason, she is fearless. All she wants to do is pick the wild grown vegetables. She crawls under all the wires, careful to avoid the booby traps.

Luom learns from listening to her father every night after supper. Bay teaches his family from his experiences. This way, they will be able to survive if danger ever crosses their path. The Police Chief never imagines his daughter will test her learning. Luom feels a need to be in on the action and luckily, some spirit must have been watching over her.

Few people like the Police Chief, but women are more attracted to him than men are. This greatly affects Luom, who is older now. In school, many children dislike her; she is a lost little girl.

All the students begin practicing a song for the upcoming holiday event at the Mayor's building in the next town. Unfortunately, Luom's loud voice overpowers the other childrens' and makes them uncomfortable to sing with her. Although concerned about the sound, the teacher does not bother to correct Luom. Instead she purposely misinforms Luom, saying the trip will begin at 8 a.m. They leave early next morning at 7 am without her.

Luom arises and dresses in her best: a dark blue skirt and white blouse. At exactly 8 a.m., Luom shows up at the front of the school. The grounds are empty. Confused, Luom patiently sits, stands and finally walks around the school by herself, waiting and waiting. Much later, the restaurant owner from across the way comes across the road to speak to her.

"They have been gone since 7 o'clock," he says.

Luom feels badly mistreated; she cannot understand why people would trick her this way. She becomes angry with herself. Unsure what to do next, Luom remains in the schoolyard, distracting her mind with Hop Scotch until noon. Then, she heads home.

Entering the house, she acts as if she has just returned with the school group. However, Mrs. Danh is not deceived; she knows something is wrong. If Luom had gone on the trip, she would not have come back this early. Despite this reasoning, Mrs. Danh decides to ignore it and let Luom deal with the situation in her own way. Changing into her regular clothes, Luom folds her outfit puts it away, knowing she likely will never put it on again.

The following morning, remembering the events of the previous day, Luom decides to skip school. She lies on the hammock beside her brother Dung, singing him to sleep. Poor brother Dung, how could he rest when he has to listening to his sister's extremely loud, earsplitting voice. Instead of going to sleep, he lies in the crook of her arm, staring into her face. Luom sings as loud as she can, so that everyone can hear her. The song becomes more of a slurred shout than a sung melody. It reflects Luom's anger at herself. Why doesn't she ever fit in anywhere? Dung tells his sister, "You are hurting my ears."

Luom says, "Be quiet. Listen."

Dung has no choice other than to stick his fingers in his ears, attempting to shut out her loud voice.

In the private school next to her house, the students and the teacher hear Luom singing. They are amused. They know that she should go to school like everyone else instead of staying home to sing. Yet, laughing at her, they clap their hands loudly every time the song ends. Luom thinks she is good.

A month passes by and still, Luom stays home. She tells Ba Di Nam, "You don't have to put Dung to sleep. I will."

Ba Di Nam asks Luom, "Now, what are you up to?"

Luom doesn't answer her great-aunt, but instead grasps Dung, hauling him off Ba Di Nam's arm. She resumes her place on the hammock and begins to sing.

Mrs. Danh finally asks her daughter, "Why aren't you in school?"

Luom pauses to answer her mother, "They didn't have a place for me to sit." Focusing on Dung, she continues her singing.

Mrs. Danh looks at Luom, "What a quack."

"I'm not lying to you Nanny. My chair is too big, it doesn't fit in there."

Mrs. Danh becomes angry with Luom for answering her in

such a manner. "Luom, why won't you try to be normal like other children?"

"What do you mean Nanny? This is as normal as I can be."

Mrs. Danh demands, "Tomorrow, I want you to go back to school."

Luom again back talks, "I told you Nanny, they don't have room for me."

Mrs. Danh realizes if she stands there any longer, she will just become more upset. She gawks at Luom for a few more seconds, and then walks away.

Chapter 14
Mother is Concerned

The weather is usually hot and humid before the rainy season begins. Yet, in spite of the heat, Mrs. Danh asks Luom to go to the market for her. Lacing her voice with the utmost politeness and consideration, Mrs. Danh inquires, "Would you like to go to the market for Nanny?"

Luom is unenthusiastic about the task, but Mrs. Danh's rarely warm and loving tone wins her over. "Come on baby, do it for Nanny. Please."

She is begging more than demanding. Luom falls down in a fit of laughter. She knows her mother's unnatural sweetness must come of a great effort. Cutting short her laughter, Luom takes advantage of the situation, challenging her mother, "Nanny, if you give me some money to eat in the restaurant, I will do it."

Mrs. Danh smiles and answers, "I will, but never let your father see you in the restaurant. You know he forbids girls and women in this family to eat outside of home."

"Nanny, you know I do it all the time."

Mrs. Danh again smiles down at her daughter, and in an even more polished tone says, "Nanny will give you enough for two bowls of soup!"

Luom walks in the direction of the market, soon realizing she must pass by the principal's house. As she approaches, she shields her face with the coconut foliage hat she prepared before leaving, her head toward the ground.

The principal peers through the window. Even though the big coconut hat seems to have swallowed her whole little body, he still recognizes her. Arms curled against his chest, he comes out of his house to stand in front of her, blocking the way. Luom is forced to look up at his giant figure when she walks straight into him. Taking a step back and bowing, Luom says courteously, "Hello, Principal."

Wasting no time, he says to Luom, "This Principal wants his student back in school."

Luom's head remains tilted toward the dirt as she answers, "Principal, I do not want to go back to school. Everyone is cruel to me."

"You go back to school. Don't give up for this reason. Come back, things will be different."

"Principal, how will it be any different?"

"You'll see."

Luom still tries to make an excuse, "People don't like me because of my father and who I am."

The Principal seems to understand what Luom is going through and to care deeply. "You are facing challenging times at your young age. You'll do well later in life. Do not let this bring you down."

Finally looking up at her Principal, Luom sees that he means well. With renewed energy, Luom nods her head. "Yes!"

Smiling and excited, he asks, "You will?"

Luom again nods her head. "Yes!'

"See you tomorrow."

Early at dawn the next day, Luom gets ready for school. Mrs. Danh is happy and surprised; she wants to encourage her daughter. "I will double your allowance from now on."

Luom cheerfully looks to her mother. "Really, Nanny?"

"Yes! Definitely."

Luom enjoys her mother's show of love. Maybe, she thinks, she should do this more often. She heads to school in a truly happy state without any concern of possible troubles awaiting her.

When she reaches the school, Luom is unprepared for the change. Again, she faces loneliness. This time no one even looks at her.

They treat her differently, alright; they stay away from her more than before. However, Luom remembers her promise to the principal that she will stay in school. She must keep her word.

The monsoon season begins and the rain pours down for days and nights. Water floods everything, and the sky is always a gloomy stretch of sweeping gray. At recess, the children have no place to play, other than on the porch. One of the boys plays with a coin, He drops it and it rolls to Luom's foot. Not feeling at all friendly, Luom kicks it out into the rain.

The boy's sister screams at her. "Pick it up and give it back to him!"

Luom flashes a hateful look at the girl. Narrowing her eyes, she merely said coldly, "Pick it up by yourself!" then turns on her heel and walks away.

The situation worsens. Luom is constantly in trouble. Because she no longer cares what people think, she is the one now causing problems. Everywhere she goes, people seem either to be afraid of her or to whisper behind her back. Luom hears them murmur, intense dislike mirrored in their faces as it is on hers. Even some of the teachers are cold towards her. They treat her unfairly. She didn't start this problem; it was all because they detest her father.

Luom often catches glimpses of the principal's face through his window. It is always filled with disappointment, for though his intentions are from the heart, perhaps they are not for the best. His outward appearance further worsens the matter, causing others to believe he favors the daughter of the Police Chief. Luom is frustrated and she tries to find a way to deal with the situation. Finally, she comes upon a solution to keep herself distracted from her problems.

Every morning, after Mrs. Danh gives Luom money for breakfast and lunch, Luom goes to her grandfather, Mr. Ngoc, to receive some more. She then runs up to her father and puts her hands out, asking for the same. Between the three of them, Luom has plenty to spend. Yet none of the money is used to fill her stomach. Instead, she pays the boys to go to the grass field and catch butterflies for her. This new hobby of collecting butterflies keeps her busy and she enjoys watching the boys run around at her command. When it comes time for food, she will have no money, but Luom thinks of a way around this problem. She will merely show up at one of the food stands, and when the owner asks if she wants some food, all she must do is nod her head. She will have a full belly.

Every first and fifteenth of the month, Mrs. Danh visits the entire food court in the village to pay her daughter's debts.

Luom's behavior disturbs the whole town, and even her principal no longer tolerates her decisions. He and one of the teachers decide to visit the Police Chief. They talk for several hours. A few days later, the Police Chief enrolls his daughter in the private school next to their house.

Luom happens knows some of the kids who moved from her previous town' school. Her new teacher is an old man. Everyone knows he is very strict. His name is Thay Giao Thieu. He brings out the best in his students, encouraging them to respect one another. Thay Giao Thieu teaches three important subjects: mathematics, reading, and writing. These are assigned every day. However, there is no homework; students do everything in the classroom. He teaches everybody in only one classroom, grades first to eighth. After students finish their work, they must exchange their work in pairs, boys with girls. If anyone makes a mistake, they all take turns whipping each other. The discipline is embarrassing, but at least students can choose their partner.

One boy, Chau, who catches butterflies for Luom, is attracted to her. Knowing this, Luom believes he will make a good candidate with which to exchange papers. She walks up to his desk and hands him her work.

"If there is a mistake, don't whip me so hard."

Chau asks, "Then would you do the same for me?"

Luom lightly moves her head up and down to indicate agreement, and then returns to her desk to check his work. Their plan does not deceive their teacher, who has many years of experiences and is now old and wise.

The time comes to trade papers. Luom and Chau have both made two mistakes. The classroom is silent. Not even the drop of a pencil or the turn of a page disturbs the quiet. Thay Giao Thieu watches them, then takes the whip out of the desk and gives it to Chau.

Chau raises his arm and brings the whip down gently. Now it is Luom's turn, and the classroom is suddenly noisy. Some clap their hands, others bang on the desks, and the teacher's voice is loud and clear.

"Make sure you whip him hard. If you don't, I'll whip you. Your father had a long talk with me and gave me permission to teach you. Other teachers might be afraid to touch you, but I'm not."

Luom looks at her classmate still lying on the floor as she hears the words and makes her decision. Her arm swings high, and not wanting to see what happens when she brings it down, she shuts her eyes tightly. The whip cuts hard through the air. Each time the bamboo stick comes down, Luom's heart is in pain just as her friend's buttocks must be in pain. Her stomach is rolling. Two lashes for two mistakes.

A stream of tears rolls down Luom's face. Chau is hurting and everyone is laughing. The teacher looks down at Chau.

"Dumb boy, this will teach you. Next time, never listen to a girl again, especially her."

Luom promises herself never again to make any deals. Chau stays away from her for weeks.

After that incident, Luom gets herself into more trouble with the teacher. Thay Giao Thieu commands her to use a dip ink pen to write on her paper, and often Luom makes it messy. Thay Giao Thieu becomes angry and to discipline her, hits both of her palms with the ruler. For each splotch on the paper the ruler will go down on her small hand. Every day she returns home with hands red and sore.

One day, Luom comes home with ink covering her clothes. She had spilled the whole jar of ink on herself. That morning the teacher's ruler broke from hitting Luom's hand so hard. Even so, Luom hides her hand from everyone in her family by sticking them in her pockets or behind her back.

School gets out for three months of summer. In the second month, Chau comes back to ask Luom if he can catch more butterflies for her, telling her she will not have to pay. All of the boys reappear with him. Happily, the group plays with Luom in front of her house.

One afternoon, while Luom waits for the boys to show up, she notices an old woman picking weeds in front of her father's courtyard. Curious, she asks the old woman, "What will you do with these?"

The old woman answers Luom, signaling with her hands. "This

is my food."

Luom thinks this is a strange way to answer, but quickly realizes the old woman is mute. The woman gives Luom some of the weeds to take home to cook. Luom is surprised when it turns out to be a very tasty dish. In no time, they become good friends. They spend time together in the morning sometimes until 2 o'clock in the afternoon or whenever the boys show up.

That summer the opera returns to town for an annual performance. The owner of the show comes to visit, asking Mrs. Danh to set up an appointment for him to meet the Police Chief. The owner needs the Chief's permission to set up the opera stage. Luom attaches herself to her father, wanting to inspect the operation. She is impressed with all the people in show business.

Out of nowhere, four little girls come to ask Luom for a free ride to the show. Luom agrees, telling them to return after the sun has set. Her father always teaches her to do good for others, and now she can. But the good Luom is about to do will soon ruin her father's reputation.

Chapter 15
The Cost of Friendship

At sunset, all the girls wait for Luom at the back of the tent. They linger, watching for the start of the show. When Luom arrives, she pulls out a razor and cuts a two-foot long gash in the side of the tent. Quietly, the four girls enter. Luom thinks she has outsmarted the adults. After her friends have crept through, Luom holds the gash open with one hand and proceeds slowly inside. Suddenly, before she has a chance to stand up, she feels someone grab her hair and twist it, pulling her up straight and spinning her around.

"Why are you cutting my tent?"

Although Luom's head is wreathed in pain, she has enough sense to recognize this man's voice. Still, Luom is too shocked by what is happening to her to answer.

One of the kids answers for her: "We wanted to get in."

The owner points a finger at Luom. "Your parents are going to pay for this! We're going to the Police. Who are your parents?"

He looks down at her. Luom, gazing steadily into his eyes, wonders why people always look to her whenever something goes wrong. Luom doesn't want to tell him who her father is, but one smart-aleck girl standing beside her boasts, "Her name is Luom and her father's the Police Chief. Do not harm her or he will put you in jail. That is his Princess. No one in this town dares to harm her. You better let us go and we won't tell him that you grabbed her hair."

80

Luom grinds her teeth and shoots the girl a look that says, "What are you saying? My ass is going to be red tomorrow!"

Yet Luom's words are unable to pass her vocal cords; she is completely silent the entire time. The man squints at her until recognition slowly dawns on his face. His tone softens as he says to Luom, "Tomorrow night, make sure you come to see me."

Five front row seats are set up especially for Luom and her new friends. Better yet, the man has someone bring snacks for each of them. Repeating himself, he quietly tells Luom, "Tomorrow night, make sure you come to see me."

People around the girls, whisper to one another, sarcasm twisting their voices, "Ooo, Ooo, look! That's the Police Chief's daughter."

Luom, ignorant of the mockery in their words, is proud to hear them speaking of her.

The next day Luom learns that the show's owner has just finished a visit to her father. Fearing the worst, she hides from the Chief until noon when she cannot avoid him any longer. As part of her daily routine, she must remind her father it is time for lunch. Luom usually hangs around in front of her father's office at 11:30 am, eager to bring him home so she can meet the old woman by noon. She would have busted into his office and pulled his hand to walk home if she could.

But today, Luom leaves the dear old woman alone. At exactly noon, she shows up at her father's office, and, peering into the window, checks to see if anyone else is there. There is no one else, just the Police Chief at his desk, intent on his work. With a refined, but fearful manner, Luom knocks. Her father looks straight at her and says, "Father's loving little daughter! Come in and close the door."

Listening carefully, Luom detects that his voice is unusually gentle. She suddenly becomes more anxious. As she walks in, the Police Chief's face abruptly changes from warm to cold.

"Sit down," he commands in his deep-toned voice.

Luom can hear her heart beating as loud as the Viet Minh pounding their drums during battle.

"Yes Father!"

She sits timidly in the chair, knowing there is nothing she can do now to stop what is to come. Continuing his writing, the Police Chief asks his daughter "Is there anything new?"

Luom gulps nervously, and realizing her situation, confesses, "Yes father, last night I damaged the show tent and got caught."

Infuriated, her father looks fixedly at her. Luom glues her eyes on the floor. The Police Chief asks his daughter in an angry voice, "Don't you know that is wrong?"

"I didn't know before, father. But now I realize what I did was wrong."

His face red like a boiled lobster, Luom's father barely controls his temper, "Why didn't you know before? Why now?"

Luom is terrified to see her father fuming at her, but is just able to answer. "Because you're upset after the show owner came to see you, so then I knew what I did was wrong."

The Police Chief realizes he is frightening his daughter when he sees the way she is behaving. He softens his voice, "I had to apologize to him, so that he would extend his business for two more weeks. That means I have to make sure they are safe during that time. Do you understand?"

Blubbering, Luom answers her father, "Yes Father!"

"Yes what? I didn't hear you."

Luom's voice rises up a little higher. "Yes! I understand what I did was wrong. I'll never do it again."

The Police Chief seems to calm down, "I hope all this will be for a good reason. Our town needs some entertainment one in a while. The man has asked all of you to come back, but I think it should be only you."

Luom answers, "Yes Father!"

Realizing she has passed the punishment for now, she returns to her normal self. She grabs his hand and drags him with her all the way home. They are late for their lunch, and everyone is waiting.

Mrs. Ho Thiet asks her son, "Why are you late?"

"I had so much work to do," her father says. They all sit down to eat, acting like nothing happened.

That night, Luom attends the opera alone. She sits by herself in the special seat and eats the snack the owner provides for her. She wants to go home and end this situation. Yet, before Luom left home, her father insisted she stay to be an audience member as long as the opera is in town. If she is not in attendance, the owner will think the

Police Chief holds a grudge.

Three nights Luom sits alone, feeling more punished than rewarded. All the girls who wanted to be Luom's friend before all avoid her now.

Unfortunately, the two week extension of the opera causes the Police Chief problems of his own. On the fourth night, an undercover man comes to inform him that a problem will occur if he goes to the opera tent for his daily security check. He must cancel the show. Despite the warning, the Police Chief decides to keep his promise to the owner. He calls Luom over.

"Luom, I want you to stay home tomorrow. Do not follow me into town. You do not have to attend the show anymore. Understand?"

"Yes, father."

Luom is glad to be released from her punishment, but she feels something important is about to happen and she wants to be there. She realizes her father would never tell her to stay home otherwise. She plans to follow him in the morning.

Early the next day, the Chief and his men go to observe the situation at the market. Luom waits for her father out of sight, following him stealthily. She watches as the market fills with an abnormally large number of strangers, standing elbow to elbow.

Dozens of soldiers surround the Chief, wondering if something will happen. The Police Chief talks with one stranger who is asking for permission to open a new business. The stranger expresses his admiration of the Police Chief, saying what a good job he has done for the village. Suddenly, the man thrusts his hand forward, forcing a blade into the Police Chief's side. Reacting quickly, the Police Chief grabs hold of the man's hand and, twisting it back, takes the knife away from him. Angrily, he shouts, "You have the guts to stab me!"

Blood stains his shirt. The soldiers in a flash push the man down onto the ground, secure him, and take him away. People are running around pointing and screaming as if they are the ones who have been stabbed.

"Troi dat oi! (Heaven and Earth) Someone just stabbed Chief Bay!"

The crowd continues to erupt in screams. Luom, mouth wide open, stares at her father, frozen. Meanwhile, the soldiers carry their boss to his Jeep. One of the soldiers notices Luom and, recognizing her, snatches her from the crowd. They take her back to her house. She gets out of the Jeep as her mother gets in. Together, they drive to the hospital. While he is on his way to the hospital, his assailant informs an Assistant Police Chief that there will be an attack on their compound at nightfall. Everything happens all at once: the Opera is cancelled. Without the Police Chief, there will be no performance. The whole town is in turmoil. Some feel sorry for the Chief. Others, especially those on the side of the Viet Cong, feel only hatred. Some say he deserves what he got.

Chin Bong, Mrs. Danh's ninth sister, instructs each person to take one child and leave the house before sunset. KiKi stays behind with Grandfather Ngoc and Bay Thoi, Mrs. Danh's seventh brother.

At 8 o'clock that night, Chin Bong and Luom are the last to leave the house. Luom's aunt decides they should crawl to avoid being seen by the Viet Cong. Chin Bong notifies the military police from the watchtower before they head out.

Creeping on their stomachs, the pair moves their arms and legs as if they are soldiers out on the battlefield. The road is covered with jagged rocks and tar, making it very difficult to move. Slithering through the night on this rough surface, they still feel fortunate that the sun is not out to melt the tar. If so, their skin would have burned and the tar would have covered their bodies. Already their clothes are torn and scratched by the sharp rocks.

It takes them half an hour to get to Nam Canh's house, Mrs. Danh's fifth brother. As they arrive, the Viet Cong begins to call the soldiers to surrender. Luckily, even in darkness, Mrs. Nam, Nam Canh's wife, spots Luom and Chin Bong. Swiftly, she opens the door. When they finally get in, Luom realizes all her siblings are present.

Luom's parents often review their side-by-side fight at the Vinh Binh battle: the many scars on the Police Chief's body from his years in service; the survival methods he taught them. Mrs. Danh puts Chin Bong in charge when she is away. Chin Bong does a good job of managing the situation.

It is pitch black as they move around, feeling with their hands before making their way forward. If they want to exchange information, they must whisper into one another's ear.

Unfortunately, nature calls to Luom. She quickly walks to the restroom with Chin Bong. The restroom is built far way in back of the house on top of a muddy lagoon. Rough tree branches lie across the hole, aligned side by side next to the step entrance. Luom lowers her pants and prepares herself to go. As she begins, from somewhere below she hears a muffled curse, "*Dich Me!*" (My mother's fart) Luom realizes someone must have been looking for a place to hide, and had stupidly chosen the bathroom pit.

Scared stiff, Chin Bong gasps loudly and rudely yanks Luom out of the restroom. As she pulls Luom away from the swearing man in the waste pit, Luom tries to pull up her pants. Chin Bong drags her towards the entrance, forgetting about the footsteps in front of them. Chin Bong plunges past the obstacle, but Luom is not so lucky. She blunders over it and falls on her face with her pants still down. Chin Bong is oblivious to her niece's embarrassing state and drags her across the rough tree branches, up towards the main house. Luom is in pain, but there is no time to think about it.

Both sides begin to shoot. The air, alive with bullets and rockets one moment, is silent the next, until the shooting erupts again. It is just like all the battles Luom has seen before. While everyone else fears for their lives, Luom enjoys the excitement, having experienced this before. She is fearless and feels like a professional, surrounded by her family.

Meanwhile, at home, eighty year-old Grandfather Ngoc is unable to find his way around in the darkness to the shelter. He accidently stumbles into the corner of the door and after recovering from the pain, hurts himself again moving in the same direction. Bullets whiz by in all directions, barely missing him. Bay Thoi keeps calling to him, "Bac Ngoc! Bac Ngoc! Are you coming to the shelter?"

Still disoriented, Grandfather Ngoc calls back, "I'll be there soon!"

Bay Thoi is unaware that Grandfather Ngoc is in trouble. He thinks that Grandfather Ngoc does not want to come down to the shelter. Grandfather Ngoc never makes it to safety, but luckily, he survives to tell the tale.

At sunrise, all leave Nam Canh's house. Thu Huong and Luom dash into the compound to collect the empty bullet shells. They assemble them into a pyramid. Both children lie flat on the dusty floor, gazing at their creative structure, happy even without real toys. Empty bullet shells, bottle caps, rubber bands and cigarette packs are enough.

One of the soldiers decides to take the bus to the hospital in order to inform the Chief that the compound has been under attack. Yet Mrs. Danh, worried about the possibility of another battle, sends the soldiers home to pick up Thu Huong and two of her sons, Diep and Tuan. Luom and Dung are left behind.

Mrs. Danh, upon her arrival at the hospital, begins to direct soldiers to their posts like a commander. Eyes flicking left and right, she walks around the hospital, familiarizing herself with everything. She orders a lockdown of all the doors and stations a guard by each.

The doctors and nurses express their dislike of the situation, but nothing can stop Mrs. Danh from trying to protect her loved ones.

At 9 pm that night, the Viet Cong knock on the door. No one dares to open it. The soldiers and Mrs. Danh, moving silently, aim their pistols at the front door in anticipation of an attack. Luckily, the Viet Cong admit defeat for now and leave. Mrs. Danh knows they will be back. She orders everyone to pack up and to carry her husband out of the back door. They stay hidden in the bushes until morning. At sunrise, a soldier goes to pick up their Jeep and drive them home.

The Police Chief is still in pain, but his responsibilities forbid him ample time to rest and heal. He walks to the compound to show gratitude to his soldiers, telling them that they are doing a good job of defending the village from the Viet Cong. He then surveys the town, inspecting the damage.

Blessed by God, the town shows no sign of trouble at the moment. The Viet Cong do not want to harm the villagers, because the majority of them are Viet Cong. They come out at nights when they need to, but otherwise, they blend in with everyone else.

The village mall becomes the communication center between the Police Chief and the Viet Cong. There, the Viet Cong post a petition demanding the Police Chief's resignation. He and his wife and kids must leave immediately. The Police Chief is angry; he shreds the list into little pieces and ignores the threat. Instead of worrying about the situation, he makes plans for Chin Bong, his sister in-law, to marry one of his men.

Chapter 16
Marriage Arrangement

Mr. and Mrs. Duong agree with the Police Chief's arrangement for Chin Bong's marriage. Yet Chin Bong refuses, because she hardly knows anything about her future husband. Mrs. Danh tries to convince her sister to accept, Chin Bong says, "Why are all of you trying to get rid of me? I don't have to marry."

Mrs. Danh answers, "Mother and Father think a girl should be married before twenty one years of age."

"I'm not going to."

Mrs. Danh stomps over to her sister and slaps her across the back. Now thoroughly upset, with tears in her eyes, Chin Bong packs her bag to go home to her parents. Unfortunately, after reaching home, her parents push even harder for her to obey. Chin Bong fights the arranged marriage all the way up to her wedding day and beyond. Despite her efforts, she must move in with her husband's family.

His wedding gift is his parents and three brothers. Chin Bong is expected to be the head of the household. She must work out in the rice paddies as well, and must cook and clean while her mother-in-law goes out to gamble. Chin Bong doesn't believe in being a slave for anyone, even her own family, and plans to rebel.

A few days after the wedding, she throws a fit, packs up her bags and goes home to Mr. and Mrs. Duong. Once again, her parents forced her to leave. They stay true to the Vietnamese custom: when a woman gets married, she remains with their husband and his family no matter what.

Rejected by her own parents, Chin Bong ends up at Luom's front door with her bag in hand. Mrs. Danh tells her sister firmly, "Go home with your husband. You have your own family now."

Chin Bong only smiles and tells Mrs. Danh, "Hey, you put me into this marriage, you must put up with me until my family shows up."

Chin Bong's smile hides the true reason she has returned to Mrs. Danh. After living with her sister's family for such a long time, she misses them and it is hard for her to break away. Chin Bong tells her younger sister Ut Thom, "You are having all the fun now. This household never bores me."

"Yes! I am."

Mrs. Danh has no choice but to let her sister hang around until her husband, Mr. Phat, and his family come and sweet talk her into returning home. All of this amuses Luom like a soap opera. Luom mirthfully watches her aunt's ridiculous behavior each time she leaves and returns to her husband.

Chin Bong was right. Living with the Police Chief's Family is never boring. Something is always happening. One day, the Police Chief has a visitor from the West. Ut Thom and Luom are strictly forbidden by the Chief to be present when the guest arrives. Both go upstairs and begin to search for a way of spying on him. Luom finds a knothole in the floor and lays flat on her stomach, peering down through the small shaft of light.

Crouched there listening, they find that the guest speaks some Vietnamese and the Police Chief knows some English. They both randomly alternate the languages in the conversation, showing off their ability. Mrs. Danh cooks in the kitchen with the maid, preparing a meal for their guest. Luom tells her aunt quietly, "You stay here, I'll be right back."

"Where are you going? We're not allowed to go down."

Ut Thom's harsh whispers fall on deaf ears and Luom stealthily moves to the bottom of the stairway. In a flash, she passes behind her father's back, entering her grandfather Ngoc's bedroom where her parents keep all their personal belongings. Luom finds her mother's makeup kit and spreads what she can across her face, inexperienced in the art but nonetheless eager to beautify herself. In the darkness of the room, her face looks white as a clown.

Luom confidently strides out of hiding and, standing before the man, speaks the only English word she learned from her father.

"Hello!" she says brightly as she extends her hand toward the man, mimicking the actions of her father moments ago.

The Police Chief's face turns cherry red as Mrs. Danh's face slowly pales, her jaw gone slack. The soldiers in the room, serious a moment ago, break into uncontrollable fits of giggles.

Luom continues in Vietnamese, "When I grow up, I will marry you."

What she really meant to say was, "When I grow up, I will marry a man just *like* you." Somehow, the words became muddled before reaching her mouth, leading to a wild outburst of laughter from her audience. The man kindly smiles and says in Vietnamese, "*Cam on.* Thank you."

The Police Chief pulls his daughter over towards him and says something to the man in English while his hand tries to wipe the make-up off her face. He then turns to his wife. "Wash off her make-up."

Luom looks up at him, not wanting to leave, "Father."

"Come back here when you are done."

A smile lighting her face, Luom rushes off. She splashes a few drops of water on her face, smudging it even more and forcing Mrs. Danh to yank her back to wash it again. Luom returns at a run and sits next to her father. Mrs. Danh disapproves of the way her husband handled their daughter, but keeps it to herself.

After their lunch, the Police Chief takes the Western man on a tour around the village, afterward returning to the compound. The bottom of the tower holds the communication room. On the second floor, Luom's father has set up the music studio for her to sing. This allows Luom to wake up the soldiers at 6 am and remind them to stay inside the compound from 9 pm onward. At exactly 9 pm, the siren signals the beginning of curfew. Speakers are hooked up along the edge of town, so everyone can hear Luom's voice.

The Police Chief invites the man to climb the ladder to the watchtower. The view greatly impresses the Westerner, providing a nice close to the day. Both men seem to have learned from each other.

The Police Chief is unaware when he leaves that Luom has decided to climb to the lookout by herself in order to learn how to shoot a machine gun. The soldiers and Luom never really shoot; it is enough to pretend. Sometimes Luom walks around the compound from corner to corner, imagining herself as second in command to her father. Sometimes, she catches the soldiers drinking and in order to stop Luom from telling her father, they bribe her with gifts. The next day, the gifts must always be returned to their owners by order of Mrs. Ho Thiet.

While every one is having a great time, the Police Chief is unaware Grandfather Ngoc is soundless; he has been ill lately and has recently turned eighty-one. Finally, the Police Chief notices his father's silence. He takes him to many doctors. All say the same. Grandfather is very ill, old and his time is near. The doctors give up on Grandfather Ngoc.

The family stands close by as Grandfather Ngoc struggles with his last breath. Instead of crying, Mrs. Ho Thiet searches her husband's pockets for his money, asking, "Where's all your money? I'll take it before your special granddaughter Luom spends it."

Everyone in the room is annoyed by Mrs. Ho Thiet's actions, but they keep it to themselves.

Luom stands next to her great aunt, Ba Di Nam. She is terrified to witness her grandfather's dying moment. Ba Di Nam, attentive to Dung on her arm, suddenly sees her niece's face. She grabs Luom's hand and both walk slowly backwards away from the dying Grandfather, not to return for two days. The Police Chief must track his daughter down so that she can pay her last respects to her grandfather.

Grandfather Ngoc's ceremony is performed as a Chinese custom. Family members wear white garments and the memorial service continues for three days. On the last night of the funeral, the Police Chief's sisters-in-law wonder who will be Mr. Ngoc's heir, now that he is dead. They say to one another, "Must be Luom."

"Yes! Who else would have that claim?"

"Maybe your husband is."

"No, must be Luom."

As this unfeeling conversation continues, suddenly, people are struck with the awful odor of decomposition from the casket and their eyes open with horror.

The Police Chief tells everyone, "You should be ashamed of yourself in a time like this. Instead of showing sorrow for our dead father, you worry who will inherit his fortune. You all have upset his soul. If you don't stop this, I will order a soldier to escort you out." The discussion immediately ceases, not out of concern for Mr. Ngoc's soul, but out of fear of the Chief.

On the last day, all accompany Grandfather Ngoc to the cemetery. The Police Chief kneels down and bows on the ground, then takes three steps and bows again, and once again for every three steps that he takes. His siblings don't even bother to follow Chief Bay's traditional ceremony.

Villagers and families string in a line one mile long. Each villager household carries silk banners with Mr. Ngoc's name on it to show their respect. When they reach the burial ground, the silk banners are folded carefully by the carrier and placed atop his grave.

The family members refuse to leave for a long time after Mr. Ngoc's body is buried. They all head back to the Chief's house, waiting to hear of an inheritance. Mrs. Ho Thiet asks Luom, "What did your grandfather leave for you?"

"Grandfather didn't leave me anything, he has nothing."

"But you're his special grandchild. You must know where he deposits his money?"

"Ba Noi, (Grandmother on father's side) you are his wife. If he didn't leave it to you, why should he leave it to me?"

The Police Chief is furious at his mother's insensitivity and he is no longer able to stay quiet.

"Mother, Father just passed away and you didn't even shred a tear! All you're worried about is if Luom inherited his fortune! She told you, she has nothing. Father just lived here for three meals a days. Mother, please drop it, roll over and cry at least few drop. My wife will divide all the silk gifts from the village. You all can take that, we want none."

Thinking on the matter, someone says ruefully, "How could there be anything left over? Luom spent it all before he died."

The Police Chief wants nothing more than to get everyone out of his house as soon as possible. He calls out to his wife, "Danh, *Minh Oi*, would you please give everyone their share of the silk? Let me be in peace."

Mrs. Danh immediately does what her husband asks and soon everyone receives his or her share. They leave without saying goodbye. Mrs. Ho Thiet keeps asking Luom about Ngoc's inheritance, secretly, for months.

Chapter 17
Coffin

After her grandfather's death, Luom becomes even closer to the wild plant-picking old woman and spends most of her time with her. One afternoon, the old woman invites Luom into her house. Stepping in the house through the back door, Luom sees a coffin in the middle of the kitchen. Her first reaction is one of horror; the old woman's family quickly surrounds her and begins the story of why the coffin is in the house.

The old woman goes to the corner of the room as another lady tells Luom, "That's my mother in-law. She was dead for three days and she came back to life. Diem Duong, the King of Hell, forbade my mother in-law to tell what she witnessed in those three days. From that day on, she became mute. My mother in-law should have stayed dead. For her to come back from Hell, it is unnatural. This is a curse upon the next generation."

The old woman's daughter-in-law continues, "Therefore, my mother in-law is no longer living, she's a zombie. I forbid her to enter through the front door and she must sleep in her coffin. She has to provide her own food, which is why she picks those weeds. Maybe if she doesn't have enough food, she will go sooner."

Luom feels sick as she listens to the woman describe how she treats her mother-in-law. How could people be so cruel to others? Where is her son who let his wife do such a thing to his mother? Luom believes every life is recycled just as everything on Earth is. The old woman must have sinned against them in her previous life; now in this lifetime, they carry out judgment upon her.

Luom's heart breaks for the old woman, but there is nothing she can do. In order to settle her troubled mind, Luom says inside her head, "I'm sorry for what you are going through, but you must pay for your sin." Luom never returns to the dark house. Instead, she waits for the old woman daily in front of her father's office. Sometimes she arrives with a bowl of rice with fish and cups of tea in hand. Sadly, being with the old woman makes Luom miss her grandfather Ngoc even more.

One night, Luom dreams about her grandfather. She watches as he takes his hand and hits her on the head twice. The following day, her friend arrives, asking her to purchase a raffle ticket. Remembering the dream, Luom picks ticket number 55. Amazingly, on Saturday, the radio announces the number 55 is a winning number. Luom won 150 dong, which is worth about thirty dollars. It is a lot of money for Luom. Usually, Mrs. Danh gives Luom 50 cat, (one hundredth of a cent) each day. Now, in one day, she won thirty times more. Happy with this turnout, Luom thinks to herself, "Grandfather is making up for his absent money from now on."

Excited, Luom waits for her friend to come and pay her. Two weeks go by; there is still no sign of him. Despite the heat, Luom makes the trek to his house. When she reaches her destination, his parents say, "My son didn't sell to you the raffle ticket. Therefore, we don't have to pay you."

Luom walks out of their house, tears beginning to spring from her eyes. The road going home seems to stretch further with every step. When the Police Chief sees his daughter's disappointed face, he asks, "Why do you look so sad? And you didn't even come to get me for lunch. You must have missed yours."

Luom looks at her father. "Father, I'm a fool. People conned me, and there's nothing I can do about it."

The Police Chief's forehead knits into a small frown. Then, leaning back in his chair, he says, "Relax, what do you mean? Tell me."

Luom's catches her breath. "Father, I won 150 dong."

"How did you won?"

Luom is fearful of his reaction, but answers her father nonetheless. "I...bought a raffle ticket."

"Who did you buy it from?"

Sobbing, Luom says, "I bought it from my friend."

The Police Chief becomes angry with his daughter. "How many times have you heard me say that I forbid gambling in this town?"

Calling to a soldier, he orders, "Take her to get her money and come back to me at once. If they promised to pay, their promise must be kept."

Luom and the soldier arrive at her friend's house to find that his parents have changed their story. "We were going to pay you, but you misunderstood us. You took off so fast and my son couldn't catch up with you."

Handing her the money, they say, "Say hi to your parents for us!"

The soldier and Luom return home. The Police Chief has been waiting for them. "Luom, do not ever gamble again. I lay down the law; therefore, you must obey like everyone else. Is this understood?"

Knowing that her father could not stay mad at her for long, she answers him. "Yes Father!"

The Police Chief will never forget the time when he was only ten years old and had to be sold as a slave for his father's gambling debts. Seven years of servitude taught him to lay down the law. There would be no gambling in this town, especially not among his family.

The news that Luom has won money because of a dream with Grandfather Ngoc travels quickly to Mrs. Ho Thiet. In a flash, Mrs. Ho Thiet arrives on the doorstep. "Luom, why didn't you tell us about your dream? Your Grandfather has come back to give you his inheritance. Even after his death, he still thinks about you. We could all win from the government lottery."

"Ba Noi, I don't think it works that way."

"Then share."

"How much you want Ba Noi?"

"Half of it."

The Police Chief is again disgusted by his mother's lack of grief. He tells her, "Mother, you are an unusual Grandmother."

Mrs. Ho Thiet points her finger and answers her son, "Because of me, all of you are present here today, and don't you forget. So do as I ask. Besides, I am taking only half of her winnings."

The Police Chief walks away, his soul too sorrowful and weak to continue arguing with his mother.

Luom, excited about the money she won, want to share her happiness with the old woman. The next day, Luom walks to her father's office carrying another bowl of food for the old woman. Upon reaching the porch, she looks around, but there is no sight of the old woman. Luom waits and waits on the step. The door behind her opens. The Police Chief comes over to sit beside her. Looking solemn, he says, "Luom, I have sad news. The old woman will not come here to eat this bowl of rice, not today or ever again. She has passed away."

Luom is silent. Rising, she sets the bowl down beside her, bows to it, and walks away. The Chief follows his daughter home.

Luom feels rather lost with this sad turn of events. However, she chooses not to attend the funeral. Although her grandfather and the dear old woman have departed from life on this earth, she feels their spirits are nearby. Luom treasures the memories of the time she spent with them as well as the knowledge she gained from their experiences. She misses them terribly.

For three months following the Old Woman's death, Luom carries a bowl of rice to the spot where she and the Old Woman used to sit. She burns incense, saying aloud, *"Ba ve an nhe."* (Mrs, please come back to eat.)

The Police Chief respects his daughter's thoughts. Her heart is good.

Usually at two o'clock every morning, before Tuan awakens, Luom must go home to boil the water for his milk. Her fifth sibling, he is still a baby. Night after night, she walks into her father's compound, calling up to the soldier in the tower before leaving the gate, "This is Luom!"

After receiving permission, she moves quietly across the L-shaped bridge, crosses the road, and enters the front yard of her house. The door is never locked so she goes inside. She goes straight the living room and stops by the table where her family members worship her grandfather to pay her respect.

The incense must burn daily and the oil lamp is required to stay on for three hundred sixty days. To the left of the table is his bedroom. No one has slept there since Grandfather Ngoc passed away. It fills the whole house with gloom and Luom feels that his spirit remains.

The first year after they moved in, Luom slept near her Grandfather to take care of him. She became closer to him than any of his other grandchildren. Now, her parents instruct her to burn incense every time she goes to the house.

While Luom lights the incense, her hand trembles. The artist's talent seems to have made her grandfather's picture come back to life. It appears as though he is staring at her, his eyes burning into hers. Luom suddenly feels fear overwhelming her. She worries that his spirit is still angry with her for showing up late for his funeral. Luom begins talking to the picture, "*Ong Noi!* Grandfather! I come home for Tuan's milk. Please, watch over me."

On the right of the house, Luom enters the bedroom of Ba Di Nam and Ut Thom. Both women sleep with Dung, Luom's sixth brother, who is only four years old. He has serious asthma. Unfortunately, there is no medication for him. Sleeping pills are the only treatment, and some nights, even they do not help.

After passing their bed, Luom finds herself in the kitchen. She lights the wooden stove to boil the water. Still scared, Luom is clumsy as she lights the stove. She must keep puffing and puffing into the smoke to help the fire get started. With its rear on the lagoon, and its front still holding her grandfather's spirit, the house feels haunted. A chill runs up and down her back. Luom senses Grandfather Ngoc standing behind her and is terrified of his ghost. Anxious to finish making the milk, she rushes. She must return before Tuan wakes everyone up. Her father and the soldiers need their rest after patrolling the town at night.

Walking back to the compound, Luom remembers the Viet Cong could shoot her at any time.

The Police Chief often speaks with Luom about his responsibilities. He tells her he must make sure the town is safe for everyone. Businesses need to grow and he must deal with the Mayor and others. Regardless of how many people the Police Chief knows, he is a lonely man and Luom is his best friend. She keeps her father's confidences secret, never repeating anything her father has shared with her. Since Mr. Ngoc died, the Police Chief remains sad that his father's soul is lost, wandering in darkness.

Chapter 18
Pets

Some time later, someone from far away in the swampland brings the Police Chief a python and two swans. Bay instructs Luom that they are now her pets and she must take care of them. Daily, Luom goes to the market and buys rice field rats to feed the snake. The swans find food for themselves in the lagoon.

After months of feeding an ever-fattening python, Luom returns from school one day to find the snake on the dinner table. She asks her father, "Father, I thought that was my pet?"

Her father smiles and says, "It was, until he got so fat. You overfed it."

"You told me to."

The Police Chief laughs. "I did? It was my mistake."

Then he sits down to enjoy the python dinner. Luom can't refuse, because it would disrespect her father and God. The Chief always said to Luom, "When there is food to eat, you should be thankful to God. Eat what he gives." She does.

Some areas of the lagoon are very shallow, only a few feet deep. Luom enjoys the water. Her father has a little canoe made especially for her. She paddles and plays with the swans on the water. Sometimes she ends up at her grandmother's house, eats lunch and paddles back home. Mrs. Ho Thiet sets strict guidelines for Luom on how to eat, encouraging only good habits. Luom is still a young child and does not understand obedience. Nevertheless, Luom recognizes differences in the ways her grandmothers show their love towards her. While Mrs. Duong gives up everything for her grandchildren, Mrs. Ho Thiet expects her grandchildren to give up everything for her.

The hot summer days, combined with the moisture in the air, make people go crazy. Luom uses the lagoon to get away from the humidity. She practices swimming as KiKi runs around chasing the swans. With Luom's loud mouth happy and screaming and the swans excited, Kiki becomes even more enthusiastic. Yet no matter what, Kiki never harms Luom or the swans.

Suddenly, a gunshot rings out over the lagoon. Luom turns quickly enough to see Kiki's body collapse into the water. Quickly, Luom attempts to get to Kiki. Only a few feet away from her, it seems to take forever to reach him. Squatting down in the shallows, she picks up Kiki's head, just enough to raise his head above the water. Her tears pour down her face. She tears her eyes away from Kiki's matted fur and looks to the shore. Her father stands there, his face a mask of horror, barely holding onto the pistol in his limp hand as his shock begins to fade he runs down to Luom.

He grabs Luom and holds her in his arms. She realizes her father shot KiKi, thinking the dog was going to harm her. Luom looks through teary eyes at the swans, still running around in their misery. The Police Chief's eyes are red, his mistake already beginning to haunt him. It seems he has been crying ever since his father died. Now Kiki is dead by his hand, Kiki who saved the Police Chief many times in battles.

In that moment, Luom feels as if time stands still, everything around her is silent. Everyone nearby who heard the shot ran over and saw the sad pair before them. The soldiers stare at their boss. Slowly the Police Chief rises and wades into the water. Reaching Kiki, he picks up the dog and carries it to shore. Luom and her father sit next to the limp body for a long time, memories flooding their mind. Mrs. Danh finally comes over and orders the soldiers to take Kiki away.

Leaning down, Mrs. Danh puts her arms around her husband and help him stand. They lead him to Mr. Ngoc's bedroom to rest.

Luom is taken to shower. The sound of singing swans drifts from across the water. That evening, they bury Kiki's body in the front courtyard in Mr. Ngoc's garden.

Two days later, the Police Chief is no longer able to listen to the racket of the swans. It reminds him so vividly of that moment. He orders the soldiers to help the chef cook the swans. If the Mayor had not troubled the Police Chief that day, Kiki probably never would have departed from the earth and the beauty of those swans would still be on the calm waters of the lagoon.

The death of KiKi has not yet faded when before another episode happens a few days later. One of the Chief's closest soldiers, a man by the name of Mr. Tu, lost both an arm and a leg on the battlefield. Mr. Tu has nine children. With the little money he earns from the government, he is unable to support his whole family. For this reason, Mr. Tu decides to become a fisherman. One afternoon, Mr. Tu's eldest child comes looking for the Chief.

"Sir, my parents have not yet come home from fishing yesterday and my mother does not know how to swim. I am afraid something has gone wrong—my parents would never leave us this long."

Worried by the news, the Police Chief immediately orders his soldiers to gather and set out in search of the couple. However, after days of looking, Mr. and Mrs. Tu are nowhere to be found. Everyone, including the Chief, is ready to give up.

Suddenly, one of the villagers runs to the Chief. "Chief! I saw a dead body washed up at the river's edge."

The Chief drops what he is doing. "Take me there." Remembering his daughter, he tells her, "Luom, do not follow."

Nodding her head, she agrees. "Yes, father."

Soon after the Police Chief leaves with his soldiers, Luom begins to trail her father. Thu Huong wants to tag along. Luom cautions her, "You've got to keep quiet—no talking or father will hear us."

"I will."

Luom, trying to keep up with her father's speed, drags Thu Huong with no mercy.

When they reach the river's edge, they see a large crowd gathered. Thu Huong and Luom are terrified when they see Mr. Tu's body. It is almost unrecognizable, yet everyone knows it is Mr. Tu. A big man, six feet tall and big boned, he stood like a giant over other Vietnamese. The body is missing the right arm at the elbow and the left leg at the knee. There is no mistaking it. The left arm lies above the head, the right is midstroke. It reminds Luom that Mr. Tu was a good swimmer, even after the loss of two limbs. Some said they saw him practicing and soon the theory developed that he had tried to save his wife and she pulled him down with her.

Luom quietly asks Thu Huong, "Does it scare you?"

"Yes! It's awful. I don't think I will sleep tonight."

"Why don't you go home then?"

"Sister, I don't want to."

"Then should we go see Mrs. Tu's body too?"

"Yes! Make sure you hold my hand, sister."

"I think you need to go home."

Thu Huong shakes her head and thrusts her lips out: "No."

Both again follow their father and the group of people to a different part of the river. Mrs. Tu's body lay not far from where her husband lay. Her hand gripped the air, as if she had been trying to hold on to something. The Chief's loud voice broke the still air as he ordered his soldiers, "Have their coffins built."

"Yes, sir."

The soldiers hurry away to carry out their assignment. An hour later, their coffins are finished and brought down to the river's edge. For Mrs. Tu's small form, the coffin is premade, but for Mr. Tu's large size, the coffin must be build specially.

Sadly, people shy away from the smell of decomposition and only a few attend the funeral. All of the donation money is brought to the Police Chief to help the Tu's children. Because their bodies are decayed, the Police are unable to have the usual three-day ceremony. There is just enough time for the children to have a last moment with their parents, and then the bodies are buried the next day.

Death lies on the water in the form of the couple, KiKi and the swans. Luom is no longer interested in learning how to swim or row her boat. The lagoon remains empty of the little canoe that carried Luom around on the water and the flitting shadows of swans no longer chased by KiKi. Luom lives in a nightmare of these images every time she nears the water. She has trouble sleeping. Thu Huong stays close to

Mrs. Danh to shield her from the dead.

Dreadful things seem to happen to the Police Chief at every turn. The threat of the Viet Cong is never far from his thoughts. The only way Chief Bay feels he can escape his present life is by having affairs with other women. One woman is married and her name is Ba Tich, a friend of Mrs. Danh. When Ba Tich's husband returns from jail, she wants to end her relationship with Chief Bay and go back to her husband. Chief Bay tries to keep Ba Tich with him. His domineering forces Ba Tich to go to Mrs. Danh for help.

There is also a young woman by the name of Dao. Miss Dao is pregnant with Chief Bay's child. She asks Mrs. Danh to accept her into the family as Chief Bay's second wife. She tells Mrs. Danh that her family up in Sai Gon is very rich and could help the Chief's career as well as take care of his whole family. Kindly, Mrs. Danh tells her, "Miss Dao, you're young. You have your whole life in front of you. Forget about my husband and go back to Sai Gon to start your new life."

Mrs. Danh brings the issue to her husband's attention, cuddling their son Tuan on her arm as she speaks. The other children stand by waiting for her to put them to bed. As she nears the end of her explanation, the fury burns bright in the Chief's eyes. Reaching toward his uniform, Chief Bay draws out his pistol and points it at Mrs. Danh's head, threatening to shoot her.

Mrs. Danh stares into her husband's eyes, and realizes he has gone crazy. Seeing the evil within him, she says nothing further. She quietly signals for Luom to hold tightly onto her little red bag of money and gold. Mrs. Danh takes Diep's small fingers in hers, and all the children slowly inch backwards.

Chief Bay calls out to Luom, "Luom, come here with me. Let them go."

Fearful of her father, Luom grasps the red bag even more tightly, not wanting to lose it. She shakes her head, her face in tears. Her action clearly shows that she is taking her mother's side.

Her father shouts at her, "Get out of here! I don't need you!"

Mrs. Danh turns around, pulling Diep behind her and moves away fast. Thu Huong and Luom run behind their mother. Together, they all head to Mrs. Ho Thiet.

Mrs. Danh is no longer her mother in-law's favorite. Mrs.

Ho Thiet worships her son as a king, remembering that he has saved everyone in the family and brought them through many hardships. It does not matter who he hurts. He has suffered with them, and still provides food for the table. Whatever or whomever Chief Bay wants, Mrs. Ho Thiet agrees with him. In addition, Chief Bay's mistresses have been showering Mrs. Ho Thiet with plenty of gifts. Dignity is no longer within Mrs. Ho Thiet or her relatives and she doesn't mind how many wives or mistresses her son cares to keep.

When Mrs. Danh and her children show up on the doorstep, Mrs. Ho Thiet is sitting in her front room chewing tobacco. Glancing up, she asks her daughter-in-law, "Why are you all here? Stay at home and deal with your husband. You don't know how to keep your husband happy! He has to find someone else! You should be ashamed of yourself. He should be able to have as many wives as he pleases."

Mrs. Danh did not care about what her mother in-law says. She cares only to keep her children safe. She refuses to involve anyone other than Mrs. Ho Thiet. Uninvited, Mrs. Danh and the children push their way into the house. As for Luom, the words of her grandmother ring in her head and she sits on the front door step alone. Whining mosquitoes pick at the poor girl.

At eleven o'clock that night, Chief Bay sends one of his soldiers to escort Mrs. Danh and his children home. Mrs. Danh stoutly refuses and Police Chief Bay has no choice other than to come in person. He begs his wife to return home. Meanwhile, his mother tries to put more heat into the situation.

"Yes! Take your *queen* home. We are poor here. We're unable to make your *queen* comfortable."

Disregarding his mother's words, the Police Chief continues to beg his wife to come home. Looking at her children, Mrs. Danh realizes she must take the chance of going home with her husband. It is too dangerous to stay with Mrs. Ho Thiet because of the threat of the Viet Cong. Although their lives are in danger either way, at least they might be able to survive with her husband. She begins to feel that maybe her husband is no longer a threat to her and the children. Nodding at him, she agrees to return home. Before they leave, Mrs. Ho Thiet says her last word to her daughter in-law and her grandchildren, "Please! Do not come back here again. We barely have enough room and food for ourselves."

That night Luom goes home in fear of her father, the image of his gun pointed at her mother's head standing clearly in her mind. She refuses to be around him. He sees this and tries to make up with better behavior.

The next day, while dining, Chief Bay asks Luom bluntly, "If your mother and I divorce, who would you like to be with?"

The bitterness at her father wells up inside of her. Luom coldly points at her mother and answers, "I'll be with Nanny."

Chief Bay seems hurt by his daughter's answer. It is not what he wants to hear. Luom is truly like a friend to him, a daughter who is like a son. She has always been devoted to him, and walks where he does. He knows he has asked his daughter a vicious question, but he will not admit his own fault. To cover up his humiliation in front of everyone, he says coldly, "Your answer should be, 'I'll not be with either of you.'"

Luom bows her head to her father. With a wounded heart, she softly answers, "Yes, father, I'll remember. I'll not be with either of you. I'll be by myself."

Chief Bay is pleased with his daughter's answer, which he follows with his loud laugh, believing he has reestablished his order. In his mind, Luom is soft and weak and he knows she will obey. Everyone present, however, thinks Chief Bay is kidding.

Except Mrs. Danh. She knows her daughter more than anyone else did. Luom is a very stubborn child, even when she doesn't show it to her father.

As for Luom, she tells herself, "Go ahead and end your marriage. I'll do exactly what you say."

Luom has heard the rumor that the First Lady, Madam Ngo Dinh Nhu, does not recognize divorce. Therefore, she knows that if her father or any other man wants to end their relationship, they simply walk out on their wife and kids. This knowledge makes Luom even more resentful.

Chief Bay realizes his daughter disapproves of his actions, but he is unaware that she is embittered. He doesn't know she has been keeping score of everything he and his side of the family does.

Meanwhile, Chief Bay breaks away from Ba Tich and decides to let her return to her husband. Miss Dao too leaves, taking Mrs.

Danh's advice and moving back to Sai Gon to start her new life. It remains unknown what Miss Dao will do with the baby she carries.

Yet Chief Bay does not lose much. He still has many other concubines. As a Police Chief, he is in charge of many villages, and it is rumored he keeps one in each. Who knows how many children he fathered? Chief Bay already brought home one woman before his father passed away and she became another of Mrs. Danh's best friends after being introduced by her husband. Everyone calls the woman Mrs. Tam Chi. She was about to walk away from her marriage and shave off all her hair to give herself to Buddha, but stopped when she found her childhood lover, Chief Bay.

Mrs. Danh has no other choice than to accept Tam Chi into her family as a sister. Tam Chi brings so many gifts that now everyone is blind. Luom refuses to accept any gifts from Tam Chi. Her mother understands her daughter's actions, but warns her.

"Luom, I know you don't like this arrangement. However, if you do anything to cause difficulties in this situation, your father could kill you. Think. Please."

Luom is now only 11 years old, a time when many children her age would be having fun with their friends. Yet the words, "*Your father could kill you,*" weigh heavily on her mind. With another woman in control, Luom lives on the edge of fear of her father, while everybody else around him has surrendered to it. Luom's anger towards him stirs in her stomach, rumbling darkly inside. She begins to feel as if her future is steering slowly into a tunnel with no light at the end. Luom tries to keep a distance between her and her father. She remembers the books she read that tell how most of the men in the world are untruthful. Now, she analyzes any man before her with a skeptical eye.

In all the years since beginning his military career, the Police Chief has faced the devil every minute, from every direction. He has become a devil himself; he is no longer able to recognize right from wrong, and as Police Chief, every move he makes, even in his personal affairs, cannot be hidden from anyone. Soldiers are always present at their house. Whatever happens, the news travels quickly by word of mouth within a few hours. His activities disturb the town people and their anger intensifies. The Viet Cong put up posters daily, demanding Chief Bay and his family leaves their town.

Chief Bay refuses to back down.

Chapter 19
Fears

A few weeks later, the Viet Cong assassinate the Mayor. The horrible and painful story of his death reaches Luom's ears. It took a long time, she hears. As much as the Mayor tried to get up to escape, more bullets went through his body. The Viet Cong shot him until he was unable to stand up to walk away. His body was covered with many bullet wounds and blood was everywhere. He left behind his wife and children, who had to carry his body out of town for a proper burial.

The death of the Mayor shakes up the Police Chief. Unquestionably, he can no longer avoid another order by the Viet Cong. Chief Bay now prepares to write his resignation letter. He will post it outside of the village market, letting everyone know he is no longer in charge.

In his last few days of duty, Chief Bay calls Luom into his office and asks for her help. Actuality, he just wants someone with whom he can speak privately. Luom and her father again team up, giving them a chance to learn of one another in a short time.

In that moment, Chief Bay realizes he can't trust anyone other than his little girl. No matter what she feels toward him, she is still his daughter. Whatever he tells her, she repeats to no one.

Luom asks him, "What will we do with all these papers, father?"

"We'll make sure they are in order for the next Police Chief."

Worried, Luom wonders aloud, "Where are we going from here?"

"Well, my original plan was to go with Miss Dao to Sai Gon. She and her parents offered to help all of us. Unfortunately, your mother put a stop to that. Your grandparents taught me that men in my position need to connect with the outside world. It's common to choose a rich family and marry their daughter. They do not care if I already have a wife or many more. That is the way I stay connected. In Chinese culture, it is handed down from generation to generation. A man could have as many wives as he pleased, as long as he makes sure to take good care of them."

Luom thinks for a minute, and then asks, "Father, the ancient storytellers speak the truth? Chinese people did live that way?"

"Yes! That is how it has worked before—people must have more love to survive."

Luom is silent for a moment before she responds. "Father, I do not think I like your way of life."

"I have understood for quite some time that you disapprove of what I did. Nevertheless, this is the only way I know how to live. I live in terror, knowing those bullets could fly through my body at any time. Maybe next time it will be impossible for me to avoid death and I will no longer able to be with all of you."

"Like the Mayor?"

"Yes. Like that."

"Then, Father, you are doing the right thing to quit before it is too late."

Luom understands the Chinese culture has much influence in her family and in many others. She recognizes that her father's actions are because of the way he learned Chinese culture. She loves her father very much and recognizes that he is constantly facing death. There might even be a spy in the family. Not only her father, but many South Vietnamese soldiers must also face death the same way. Living in such a threatening time, not knowing who the enemy is or who is a friend, is difficult. Therefore, every chance the soldiers get to avoid the thought of death, they take without thinking about the consequences of their actions. Many soldiers' families face hardship on a small salary. Children grow up without their father and go to sleep hungry. Luom suddenly realizes she is not a man and has not had their experiences. Then who is she or anyone else to say what's right or wrong?

Luom feels dizzy with thoughts and turning her gloomy face toward her father, tells him," Father! I do not want to get married when I grow up or have any children. Is that why you don't want me to learn how to speak Chinese?"

Chief Bay kisses his daughter on her forehead and says, "Yes! I don't want you to marry a Chinese man, but do not be afraid. You can try to find someone who is an orphan. That way, he will have no one to take care of other than you. But this is only a theory from the life I know. A man like me is unable to escape responsibility. Everything takes money, which I don't have. Therefore, I need help from others. I hope you understand me."

Chief Bay continues, "Now, I want you to be strong. There might be another way, now that Americans are in our country. Maybe you could find an American man. Do you know what they look like?"

Luom answers him in excitement. "Are you telling me you will be proud if I marry an American?"

Chief Bay is pleased to see the joy in his daughter's eyes. "You remember our guest from a while ago?" he says.

"Yes, Father. I will find someone like that."

Chief Bay puts his finger to his lips and whispers to Luom, "But this is our secret. No one must know. Understand?"

"Why, father?"

"For a woman to be married to an American, or any foreigner, would be a shame to the family and our race."

"But father, many women have married with the French."

"Yes. They have to live in humiliation and you will face the same. When I joined the French, my name was marked by the Viet Minh. Now they call themselves the Viet Cong, but my name is still marked."

Luom addresses her father with an innocent thought. "Well, I would rather be like that than marry a man like you Father."

Instead of being angry, the Police Chief smiles and, pressing a finger to her head, says, "Traitor!"

Luom smiles and says, "You told me not to, Father."

"Whatever you choose, it will be fine by me."

The silence that surrounded the pair for such a long time is now broken. father and daughter are again happy in each other's company.

After the Police Chief writes his letter of resignation, Luom looks to see if it needs to be edited. As she looks upon his eloquent handwriting, she remembers what the old Vietnamese would say. "The Chief's handwriting, it's so beautiful, just like a dragonfly." They believed that if he were born in the ancient time, Chief Bay would have been more than Chief Bay. Yet now, he is just a police chief in charge of a few small towns, and feels trapped.

Holding up the letter, Chief Bay says, "We have to send one to the new Mayor and post one on the wall of the market."

They grab their coconut hats and walk out into the pouring rain, making for the village market. Chief Bay posts the letter on the wall as the villagers pass by, paying no attention to him. It is as if the Police Chief and his daughter do not even exist.

The monsoon season is brutal. Winds and muddy roads make it hard for them to get home. Their coconut hats keep blowing off. Chief Bay tries to help his daughter with her hat as they strain against the lashing rain.

Luom shouts to her father, "Father, where do we go from here? This is our home!"

"The last time I was in Sai Gon I asked your mother's cousin if we could stay with her. We will be there for a while."

Swinging her father's hand, Luom asks, "Father! Could I salute you one more time?"

Chief Bay cracks a tiny smile and says, "In the middle of the muddy road, in this brutal weather?"

"Yes! Father, I must."

"Then I must do the same to you."

Both stand and face each other, raising their right hands to their foreheads, backs stiff. Then they shake hands.

Chief Bay realizes his daughter is growing up, and that she is trying to capture her last memory of him. Luom feels she and her father will never be together like this again. Girls growing up in her generation often did not stay even this close to their father. It is a Vietnamese saying, "*Nu Sanh Ngoai Toc.*" It means, "Born as a girl, you belong to someone else's family."

The two get home, shaking out their coconut hats onto the patio. The family members have been waiting for them at the dinner table. An unusual atmosphere surrounds the room, the stillness choking everyone's throats. Mrs. Ho Thiet at last can't stand to be silent.

"Chief, what happened? Why are both of you late for dinner?"

The Chief rises. "Mother and everyone, listen to me. I am no longer Police Chief in this town. The new Police Chief is coming in the next two days. My family and I must move."

"I am moving too?" inquired Mrs. Ho Thiet.

"No Mother, you stay at home, and do not come to this house after I'm gone. This place is no longer ours. Promise me, mother."

"Chief, why am I not going with you?"

With a gentle voice, Chief Bay answers his mother, "Mother, your life is not threatened, just mine, my wife's and my children's. I will send for you later."

Chief Bay hands Mrs. Ho Thiet a poster with a list of names the Viet Cong left. "Here, Mother, have my brother read it to you."

Chief Bay takes a deep breath and calls out in the direction of the kitchen. "Ut Thom! Come up here! Brother needs to talk to you."

From the other room, Ut Thom runs up and stands before the Chief, "Yes? You called me, brother?"

Ut Thom is humble to him as if he had been her blood brother. Chief Bay looks straight at his sister in-law. "You need to go home tomorrow morning and ask mother and father to let you go to Sai Gon with us. Your sister, nieces and nephew will need your help."

"Yes, brother," Ut Thom replies obediently.

She returns to the kitchen and begins to pack. She must take most of her stuff with her, as it is likely she will go to Sai Gon with her sister's family.

Mr. and Mrs. Duong never say no to the Chief, even though Chief Bay is with other women. To both sides of the family, Chief Bay is a good son and brother. He never curses at anyone, even when he notices that some people in his wife's family oppose him.

Especially Bay Thoi, his brother-in-law. Bay Thoi seems to be living a double life in his house, but regardless of this problem, he gives Mrs. Danh's family a fair share of his success.

Chief Bay turns to his aunt, Ba Nam, saying, "Auntie, you have been taking care of my fifth son since he was born. I would love you to remain with him, but where we are going, the house is very small and I have no job. Please understand."

Ba Nam understands her nephew's difficulty and holds Dung closer to her. As she feeds him food, she quietly sheds tears. Mrs. Ho Thiet points her finger toward the kitchen and asks of her son, "Chief, Ut Thom's life is threatened, but not mine or my sister's?"

Chief Bay patiently responds, "Mother, please understand, she must go with us to help my wife. Mother, your life is not threatened in any manner. And no more calling me Chief."

Mrs. Ho Thiet remains silent. She knows her son has already made up his mind. She remembers the past, when her son took their family out of the danger zone. Mrs. Ho Thiet takes her son's hand in hers and says to him, "You're my king. I will obey you, and I realize my king is to go underground. One day you will rise up again for our family and for me. I am waiting." Mrs. Ho Thiet leaves before finishing her dinner.

Some soldiers dining with the Chief's family have been with him for a long time. Their faces show their sadness. They feel lost, realizing their boss will never return. One of the soldiers waits for Chief Bay, remembering plans the two had made a while back. He stands, looking at the Chief to remind him of the important matter. Chief Bay understands and calls down to the kitchen for the chef to come up. She arrives before him. "Co Tu, you have been with us for a long time. I noticed you and my soldier, Mr. Hoang, have wanted to marry. Unfortunately, we will not be here. Still I wish you both the best of luck."

Mr. Hoang and Co Tu thank their boss. For Mr. Hoang, his boss's blessing is of great importance.

Diep goes to change his clothes. A few minutes later he returns, looking rather cute in his little boy's soldier's outfit. He and Thu Huong stand in front of their father and salute, ending the evening on a cheerful note.

Two days later, the new Police Chief arrives to accept his responsibility. The house will soon have a new owner.

It is the first time Mr. Bay will sleep in the house since he built it. The heavy rain drops on the roof and the winds blow, not bothering anyone. As their last night in this house, it is time for them to reflect upon the memories it gave them, the bad and the good alike. Everyone stays wide awake. Mr. Bay tell the story of his life, and of his family's life.

Mrs. Danh and Co Tu go to the market early in the afternoon and bring a few chickens to prepare as a late night meal, and to serve as breakfast. The night gradually fills with the voices of family members on both sides.

By 4 a.m., everyone has already changed their clothes. They await the beginning of their new journey in life. By 5 am, Mr. Bay says goodbye to his mother and the others, asking them to leave before he boards the bus, not wanting people to stand waving at him. He feels it would be embarrassing and he would like to have a few last moments with his wife and children alone in the house.

The trunk that was Luom's bed for so many years is left behind for Mrs. Ho Thiet. She has already come to cart everything away. The house is now completely empty.

At dawn the bus stops in front of their house. In silence, they step into the bus. The monsoon conceals their humiliation at being forced to leave their own town. It doesn't matter what country, what style of government, how big or how strong they are, or if it is ancient times or modern times—the citizens are always in control of the situation. They can and will exercise their authority without mercy.

Luom looks at the people around her, holding onto their clothes bags, the fabric wet with rain. They have moved many times, but this time everyone is different: misery covers their faces.

Chapter 20
From Rice Paddies to Big City

Luom sits by the window, tears racing down her cheeks as she hides her face beneath her dark hair.

Mr. Bay and his wife sit beside one another, deep in thought. Mr. Bay sneaks a quick last look at his house, the office building and his compound; all still stand quiet, undisturbed. Mr. Bay knows he will never return. This place had given him power and the best home he ever had for his family. Now in just a moment, all of it vanishes from his hands.

The rain pours down, making it even more miserable when they all have to walk to the ferryboats during the downpour. They reach to shore and continue another five hour bus trip to Sai Gon. Finally, between the bus station and their new apartment lay only a few miles. Mr. Bay calls a xich lo dap (bicycle connected to a wagon that has two wheels on the back, similar to a pedicab) to carry all of their things. Exhausted, everyone walks in silence to the new home.

Mr. Bay has gone to Sai Gon often; Mrs. Danh, only a few times. Their children have never been. Luom's siblings are still young and do not show any sign of worry, though Luom, herself, is old enough to be concerned. She enjoys the city lights, absent at her old home. But as she looks at the houses, she notices that they are aligned closely together. There is no privacy.

Soaking clothes make everyone feel nervous entering someone

else's house. Mr. Bay and Mrs. Danh shake off what water they can and cautiously walk in the house. Mrs. Danh's cousin says graciously, "Come in, we have been waiting for you, although we didn't know when you would arrive. The apartment is ready for you."

The circumstances are hard on Mr. Bay who knows he will have to yield in order to survive his new lifestyle. He must be humble.

"Thank you, Chi Tu."

Later, when Luom explores her new home, she is shocked to see there are only five feet between the wall of the apartment and the wall of the adjacent house. The apartment itself is quite small as well. The front and middle rooms are twelve square feet, leaving the kitchen quite a bit smaller at twelve by five. There is no window or back door, only one way in and one way out. Luom follows her father every step he takes. Yanking at his hand, she asks him, "Father, what are we going to do for a living?"

Crouching low, Mr. Bay whispers in his daughter's ear, "Tomorrow, I'll go buy a car for us and I'll sell ceramic pots."

Luom is instantly excited. "A *car*? Can I go sell pots with you?"

Softly he answers, "No! You go to school."

The property owner's son, a monk, is Mr. Bay's nephew by marriage to Mrs. Danh, even though he is the same age as Mr. Bay. Still, the monk, who practices the religion of Hoa Hao, must call Mr. Bay his uncle. That first night Mr. Bay wishes to please his new landlord, so he settles down and listens to the monk preach. This is not the first time Mr. Bay must yield. Now, his life is full of so many difficulties that he doesn't know what to do. In the end, it will be more beneficial than not to learn of other religions.

The next morning, Mr. Bay enrolls his children in a nearby school. However, because of where they're from and how they dress, the neighborhood kids bully them. Thu Huong brings up the problem to Luom, saying, "Sister, the kids were making fun of us. They called us rice paddy kids."

"They said that to me too, but we must keep it to ourselves, understand?"

Thu Huong asks, "Why don't you want to tell our parents?"

"You don't want to trouble our parents over this little thing, do you?"

Diep added, "She is right Thu Huong. We have to tough it out."

Life in the city is very busy and crowded. It is as different from the village as day and night. Water is difficult to obtain. After rising early to take care of the young before breakfast, Ut Thom heads to the public water valve. Most times she stands in line until noon. After school, Luom goes to relieve Ut Thom so that she may eat lunch. The water comes out in a ¼ inch stream. Worried for her niece, Ut Thom bolts down her lunch as fast as possible and returns to help Luom carry the water bucket into the house. If twenty people or more wait between Luom and the water, Ut Thom waits with Luom until dark, sometimes until midnight. People sit there staring at each other. A fight would break out if someone cut ahead of another. All those hours spent waiting might only be for two buckets of water at most. Some people camp out all night just for the water.

Mr. Bay is heartbroken to see his little girl trying to carry two buckets of water on bamboo stick resting on her petite shoulders. Both cans weigh more than she is, and he can feel those cans pulling her small body to the ground. If he happens to see her in this state, he offers her his help, but, stubborn like her father, she refuses.

Whatever Mr. Bay feels, Luom knows she must learn quickly.

Soon, Mrs. Danh is pregnant again. Ut Thom stays with Mrs. Danh until she has the baby, her fourth son. Si is born in Tu Du, the biggest hospital Sai Gon.

Many months trudge by. Mr. Bay struggles in the big city and the children struggle in school, their grades a symbol of how far behind they are. Unlike her husband and her children, Mrs. Danh is happy and comfortable with her cousins surrounding her. Yet the atmosphere in the house becomes gloomy through a lack of communication.

Despite the stressful situation, Mr. Bay always finds time to drive his family to the famous Sa Lo Bien Hoa, a highway a short distance away. The Americans built it during the war. Every time they take the trip, it gives the family a moment to relax in the car, breathing in the fresh air from the window as Mr. Bay speeds along.

Unfortunately, their problems are not erased completely. Mr. Bay is unable to sell his ceramic pots and the money begins to run out. One saving grace is that Mr. Bay always has connections. He is able to move his family again. This time he takes them to a better place.

Chapter 21
Life in Cao Dai Compound

Mr. Bay associates the Cao Dai[4] religion with the city of Soc Trang. He had become a worshiper of Cao Dai when he married to Mrs. Danh. Other Cao Dai believers had helped him in the past. Now he has found a place in Soc Trang for his family.

He stops the car at the entrance of the Cao Dai religious compound where a narrow dusty road splits from the pavement. Everyone must get out of the car and walk. As they walk toward the compound, a large lotus pond looms into view. A short bridge leads to their little house, surrounded by the beauty of the lotus flowers blooming from under their patio. At the sides of the house are long narrow ponds where fish of all colors swim beneath wild vegetables growing atop the surface. Banana and coconut trees sway everywhere in the wind. A creek behind the house bubbles lazily far beyond the compound's boundaries.

The Cao Dai temple provides food and shelter for Mr. Bay's family. However, in order to maintain his privilege of staying in the compound, Mr. Bay must work hard for the Cao Dai organization by volunteering many hours of labor.

Luom's passion for the beauty of nature is revived. She feels as if she is in heaven. As she begins to explore the land, she quickly learns

---

4   The Cao Dai religion, believes in one God and that the Buddha and Jesus Christ are the same person. It was founded by Ngo Van Chieu in 1926 in Vietnam.

she can find her own food. In the afternoon, while others rest, Luom steps into the center of the creek to hunt razor clams, letting the cool water run across her feet. In the thrill of discovery, Luom doesn't even feel the pain of the bamboo thorns poking her all over her body. Once she has gathered enough clams, she walks across the bridge and carries them home.

Mr. Bay sells the car he loves so much and buys himself a motorcycle with an attached cart in the back. He will try to earn a living driving people around Soc Trang. Mr. Bay spots Luom walking home from school sometimes. When he offers to give her a drive home, she always refuses, simply because she feels deeply hurt to see her father have to support the family this way. He is like a king to her, too. But what Luom doesn't know, and what nobody else knows, is that Mr. Bay is also a Captain in the Cao Dai religious army. By now Mr. Bay speaks Chinese, Vietnamese, Cambodian, French and English. He works undercover for them and helps recruit more members.

Mr. Bay sends for his mother and his sibling. Mrs. Danh is yet again pregnant. If this child is boy, it will be her fifth son. According to superstition, it is believed that the fifth son is an evil curse. Mrs. Danh decides to terminate the pregnancy. She makes her own herbal medication. She gets what she wants, but unfortunately, it almost claims her life.

Several months later, Mrs. Danh gets pregnant again. Her last experiment forces her to keep this baby. After the boy is born, they hire a nanny who lives a few miles away. The baby will not be allowed to come home. They will visit him in hiding twice a month. They name him Hoang Huy, and he is a good-looking and healthy baby. Despite these good omens and the strong name they gave him, his life is in darkness. Superstition blinds his family.

Luom's heart breaks every time she brings money to the old couple taking care of her new brother. Luom wonders what she can do to help. One day, she suggests her parents build her a little house right next to her parent's house. This way, she can take care of him while also helping her mother. Her parents tell her no.

When Hoang Huy is sixth months old, he becomes sick, forcing the couple to bring him back to Mrs. Danh. Luom and her mother take the baby to the hospital. The doctors say he has measles and a high fever. There is no hope for Hoang Huy and Mrs. Danh must take him home. Regardless of what the doctor says, Mrs. Danh and Luom fight for his life. They turn to Chinese herb medicine. For two days, Luom runs back and forth to a Chinese herbalist.

As she gets off her bicycle back home, Luom's ears suddenly pop and sharp pain threatens to split them open. Her breath comes in short gasps. She instinctively knows her brother is taking his last breath. Mrs. Ho Thiet begins to give orders, "Make sure your brother is warm where he is going. Don't let the ants get in his clothes and don't forget to bathe him."

Luom, pain forgotten, sorrowfully answers her grandmother, "I will, Ba Noi."

The next day, everyone gathers to pray for Hoang Huy before burying him. Hoang Huy's death leaves a scar on Luom's heart. She was beginning to think of him as her angel.

Later, no one will remember where he is buried, or the other three children who died before Luom was born.

Luom often sits under a coconut tree at the back of her house, watching the water flow along the creek. She wonders what her life will be like as an adult.

Meanwhile, Mr. Bay builds rabbit cages. He turns his backyard into a rabbit farm. To feed the rabbits, Luom and Thu Huong walk to the neighboring farms, asking for unwanted vegetables to carry home. Breeding rabbits is easy, but selling them is hard. The people in Soc Trang are not familiar with eating rabbit for food. Soon, everyone in Luom's family is sick of eating rabbit. The farm shuts down after a few short months.

Local teenagers gather to socialize and get water at the lotus pond. Luom watches as people take two cans, one on each end of the bamboo stick weighing upon their shoulders. As they squat down, the cans fill with water. It looks so easy, like there is nothing to it. Luom waits until no one is around, and then tries the feat for herself. She does exactly as she saw, but unfortunately, the heavily loaded water cans cause her tiny body to lose balance. She practically throws herself headfirst into the cold water. She emerges covered with dead lotus leaves from the top of her head to the tips of her toes. Luom stumbles out of the water coughing. Embarrassing as it is, at least there is no one there to laugh at her.

Luom's daily trip from home to school is a good four miles. Every day Luom and her siblings walk together until her sister Thu Huong and brother Diep head south and Luom travels north.

The family begins to feel comfortable in the city where their identities remain a secret. If someone asks about Mr. Bay's occupation, Luom answers, "My father is a motorcycle driver."

Her life has become calmer and easier than ever before. Luom is the top student in her class, and well-liked by most people in school. She is elected vice president of her class, though she often ends up doing the work of the class president as well. Every morning, she lines up the students and pulls up the flag. When she begins to sing the anthem, everyone follows. The teachers and principal put their trust in her.

Even with all the activity, Luom still likes to sit alone during recess. Her quiet attitude soon makes her somewhat of a mystery.

One day, the class president, Thanh Van, decides to see what Luom knows about life. She arrives with her friend, Thanh Vui. "Do you know where you came out of your mother?"

Luom looks up at the girls, shaken out of her reverie. "Of course I do."

"Where?"

"My mother's butthole."

Now Thanh Van and Thanh Vui are both laughing, realizing that the smartest student in class knows nothing about a woman's life. Thanh Van says, "You do not come from your mother's butthole."

"Yes, I do."

"No you don't."

"Yes, I *do*."

"Well, why don't you go home and ask your mother, then get back to us tomorrow."

Luom goes straight to her mother when she gets home and asks, "Nanny, where did I come out of you?"

Mrs. Danh says, "You came from my butthole."

Never doubting her mother's answer, Luom resolutely returns to her friends the next day to repeat herself. "My mother said I came from her butthole."

Thanh Vui and Thanh Van look at each other and laugh again. "And you believe her?"

"That is my mother's answer and yes, I believe her."

"Luom, do you have a boyfriend?"

Well, the popular girl is supposed to have a boyfriend, but Luom doesn't, the thought having never entered her mind. She is quite a homebody.

Thanh Van and Thanh Vui continue, "Well, we do."

Luom is annoyed at her classmates' bragging and without thinking, she says, "Yes, I do have a boyfriend."

As soon as the words leave her lips, Luom stands in disbelief of her lie. Not only does she not have a boyfriend, Thanh Van and Thanh Vui certainly know she is lying. However, with sly looks at one another, they let their curiosity win out. They want to see if Luom can come up with a boyfriend. "Next Monday at the Chinese cemetery, after school, bring your boyfriend."

That afternoon, Luom walks home in fury at herself. Why didn't she just say she doesn't have a boyfriend yet? Now how was she supposed to come up with one?

As she walks across the bridge towards home, a familiar face smiles at her from the other side. Hung is a boy in Luom's chanting group whom she sees monthly at the temple. He comes from a very poor family. After his mother passed away, he left school to become a vegetable wagon man. To support his family, he works hard from dawn to dusk. Luom has always admired his strong body and strong will. His handsome face blends with his medium skin tone and clear complexion. While smiling back, Luom thinks that if she were to choose a husband, she would choose him. But she is still young, and right now she only needs someone to rescue her from her prying and wicked friends.

Three days pass by until finally Luom is brave enough to hand Hung a letter. In it, she asks him to rescue her, and tells him the whole truth of the matter. The following day, Hung answers Luom's letter and agrees to meet her friends. Before walking away, he assures her, "Don't worry; everything is going to be fine."

Monday comes up fast. Thanh Van and Thanh Vui show up in front of Luom's desk. "Luom, don't forget about your promise today."

Luom nods her head at them, "I remember."

At the end of the last class, the three girls head toward the Chinese cemetery, which is more like a park then a place where the dead are buried. Luom is nervous that Hung will not show up. It is the first time she has ever done anything like this. In her hometown, she played with boys all the time, but was never this excited. Her hands sweat. She attempts to cover them up, stowing them in the folds of her clothes. As soon as Luom and the girls reach the park, they can see that all the boys are already there. They have been waiting for Luom and her friends and are already acquainted. Thanh Van introduces everyone and it is evident that she is experienced in the matter. Luom notices, that Hung dressed nicely, showing off his intelligent face. Reading her uneasy movements, Hung takes her hand and whispers, "We'll be fine."

As the group walks, Luom begins to feel cozy with Hung and enjoys the surrounding landscape, beautiful in the afternoon light. A nearby bench, crafted with pictures of a Chinese story draws them to sit on it. One hour passes by and unease creeps upon Luom as she realizes it must be getting very late. She tells her friends she needs to go home, secretly worrying that her arrival at home will end in disaster. The lunch that her mother prepares for her each day must be cold by now, and Luom still has chores to attend to.

As she rushes home, Luom envisions everyone asking her why she is late—she'll just have to say she was borrowing a book from her friend.

Luckily, upon her arrival home, no one is upset. With no clock in the house, Mrs. Danh does not realize her daughter's tardiness.

The following day, when Hung and Luom pass each other on the bridge, Luom thinks their new relationship is at an end. Nevertheless, Hung approaches her, handing over another letter. It asks to meet behind the temple, an hour after sunset. That evening, Luom tells her mother, "Nanny, I'm going to the temple to chant tonight."

Mrs. Danh smiles and is happy that her daughter wants to be a good religious girl. She nods approvingly and says, "Good, pray for all of us."

Luom walks out of the door, calling back, "I will Nanny!"

Hung and Luom, young in their adolescence, enter the temple, not bothering to hide their blooming feelings for each other. The head woman there immediately senses that the two youngsters are up to something. At the compound, it is forbidden for opposite sexes to interact or even to meet or to smile at each other. The head woman quickly goes to inform Luom's parents, though not Hung's parents. In society's view, everything is the fault of the girl and the boys are never in the wrong.

Outside, as he sits beneath the banana trees with Luom, Hung reflects on his plan to marry her when she turns seventeen. Luom is quiet too, unable to think or say anything, only smile.

Suddenly, the sound of her grandmother's voice reaches her ears. Mrs. Duong says to Thu Huong, "Let's go home. I don't think your sister is here."

Luom looks up, seeing her grandmother standing only ten feet away. Mrs. Duong holds an oil lamp, which she suddenly shines in the opposite direction, illuminating the way home, and walks off. Mrs. Duong must have seen Luom, but does not want to make a big scene.

After Mrs. Duong's sudden appearance, Luom knows she must go home. Immediately she says goodbye to Hung and rushes off.

When Luom arrives home, Mrs. Danh and Mrs. Duong ignore her. Luom creeps safely to bed, thinking she has evaded trouble for tonight at least. At about 3:00 a. m. the next morning, Mr. Bay comes home and wakes Luom up. The interrogation begins.

"Come, sit here," he says.

Nervously, Luom does her father's bidding.

Mr. Bay's voice rings out in a deep tone, asking directly, "How old is he?"

Softly and edgily, she answers her father. "Father, he's seventeen."

A sudden release of air from Mr. Bay's mouth sounds in a sigh as he inquires of his daughter, "What is his name?"

Tense with fright, Luom answers, "His name's Hung, Father."

"Is he going to school with you?"

"No, Father."

"His parents are alive?"

"His father is still living, but his mom died in childbirth."

"His father remarried?"

"Yes Father, his father remarried."

"What is his father doing?"

"His father stays home."

Mr. Bay seems to be more disturbed than before. "Then they must be rich."

Now Luom becomes even tenser than before. "No, Father."

"Then who supports the family?"

"Hung does, Father."

"How many brothers and sisters does he have?"

"He has nine brothers and sisters, Father."

Mr. Bay is even more disturbed. "Oh! So, nine brothers and sisters, with a father and a stepmother, and no one works but him. What does he do?"

"He pushes the food wagon to deliver for the grocery store."

"Do you think you could help him push that wagon to support his family?"

Luom is botheed by her father's question. She does not realize something so simple could be so complex. To help Hung push the wagon to support his parents and his siblings? That cannot be. With renewed anxiety, Luom shakes her head, bowing it and answers, "No… no. I cannot do that."

Mr. Bay seems almost amused with Luom. "You think he is going to drop everything to take care of you?"

Luom looks up at her father, eyes pleading to help her out of the situation. Mr. Bay understands, saying, "Luom, promise me you will never see this boy again, starting now."

Relief sweeps through Luom with a tinge of sadness as she says, "Yes, Father, I'll do so."

However, Mr. Bay wants his daughter to remember her promise to him. He demands, "To remember your promise, you must attend chants nightly at the temple for a month. There, you will kneel down on your knees and read the Cao Dai Bible. Every time the name 'Buddha' appears on the scrip, you must bob down three times and burn three incenses, one by one. This you should do for one hour every night."

Luom responds, "Yes Father."

"It's hard for me to see you taking care of everything in this house by yourself, but our finances are limited for now. I am unable to get your mother a housekeeper. Everything depends on you."

"I understand, Father."

When Mr. Bay reaches the end of his lecture, it is already the usual time for Luom to cook breakfast and get ready for school. However, Mrs. Duong is still visiting, and she readies the food as Luom and her father conclude their talk. Luom walks to school that morning, a miserable feeling in her gut.

That night, after dinner, Luom carries out her sentence of chanting from the Bible. She has to read ten pages and every three words, the name 'Buddha' appears. She bobs her head repeatedly, nonstop. On her right, there is a little bell sitting on the table she must sound as well. Her left hand remains straight, angled up to the center of her chest. After a month of practicing the Bible in this manner, she wishes never to return to any temple. She tells herself, "I will stay home and pray since God and Buddha are everywhere."

Chapter 22
Responsibility of the Older Child

At noon the next day, Luom spots Hung on the bridge. She quickly turns her face to hide from his view, but the narrow bridge keeps her from doing so. After passing him, Luom glances back, noticing the longing in Hung's gaze. She turns her face away to avoid contact with his sad eyes, still filled with confusion at her apparent avoidance of him. She reflects on her earlier idea to stay friends with Hung, but remembering her promise to her father, there is no way she can continue to see him. Her father even forbids her to have any male friends. Things will no longer be as they were when she was younger. At the old village, when it was raining outside, sometimes the boys and Luom would run naked in the rain, arms outstretched like airplanes. As children, they thought nothing of it, but things are different now.

Later on that afternoon, Hung walks to the lotus pond. Focused on gathering water, Luom walks to the pond without perceiving his presence. Hung approaches her quickly, wanting to talk, but Luom quickly shakes her head and returns to the house with an empty can.

Mr. Bay catches sight of his daughter at the pond and understands her dilemma; he is aware that it will be harder for her to break away from *this* young man. Yet, Mr. Bay does not want his daughter to marry too young, for she must continue to go to school. It is important that she learn to make money on her own and never depend on any man. Mr. Bay stands awhile longer lost in thought, but he can only think of one solution. It is possible to help his daughter avoid Hung by moving away.

The next day, Mr. Bay begins to search for land. He travels to the city and learns that the government is giving away some land for military families. All that is required are the children's birth certificates and his papers from the military. After that, he may choose a lot.

Mr. Bay secretly spends a whole month with family members, building the house, the children unaware of his project. The house sits on the corner of the road at a T intersection and it is easily the biggest house on the block. One tall door faces the sunset, while the other faces the sunrise, looking out on a small pond situated amidst the greenery.

Inside the house, the floor plan is simple and open. Branching off from the front room to the left is the dining table and to the right is the guest bed. A doorway in the middle of the house leads into her parents' bedroom. Luom's bedroom is across the way, connected with a new kitchen. Upon their arrival, Mrs. Danh and the children look in astonishment at their new home.

Fresh water from the river runs into the pond in front of the house and wild vegetables grow on top, helping to filter the water. Luom is thrilled at the prospect of a water hole all to herself.

Small bridges cross over the water. The water flows smoothly about the rectangular porch. The porch stretches around the house. The view is beautiful for Luom to behold through her kitchen window, her eyes travelling to the rectangular pond and beyond to the rice paddies extending for miles and miles. Luom mumbles to herself, "It will help me to study in peace."

She knows Mr. Bay must have had her in mind when he chose this piece of land. He made sure water would surround her in a breathtaking and unforgettable view. Her father made it possible for his princess to remain in good spirits with the beauty of nature beside her. The neighborhood finds they have a new singer, Luom's voice once again melodious in the afternoon sun. Yet nothing remains as a fairytale. Once again, her father disappears and resumes the usual lifestyle to which his wife and children have attempted to become accustomed.

Now that her father is often absent from home, Luom is pushed to grow faster into maturity and becomes a responsible teenager. With her father absent, Luom quickly takes her place as head of the household.

Completing school and taking care of the family simultaneously is not easy. In addition, one of her teachers is expecting a child Because her husband is out on the battlefield, she wants Luom to help her. She has no other family members nearby. The pregnancy is a difficult one. Luom's teacher cannot walk too far. Luom not only helps her teacher to and from school, she also does the woman's housework.

Carrying her teacher on her bicycle is difficult with the summer heat constantly beating down. It is especially trying when they cross the bridge. Without regard for Luom's feelings, her teacher remains on the bicycle. Luom carefully navigates her way along the bridge, cautious to keep her teacher from falling.

Repeatedly, Luom peeks around to see if Hung is on the bridge, but there is no sign of him. Rumor says he is now up in Tay Ninh, at Cao Dai's headquarters, to practice religion. Luom wonders if his going away has anything to do with their breakup. If so, he must be feeling hurt. Hung of course knew that Mr. Bay had forbidden his daughter to see him because he was poor. He doesn't understand why Luom won't fight for their love. Most young girls would pack their bag and take off with their lover, or give themselves to Buddha or commit suicide. Yet Luom chose none of those options, measuring the love of her parents as greater than that of a young man whom she just met. Luom never sees Hung again.

At school, the teachers allow Luom to act as a teacher on a regular basis. Most of the students in Luom's classroom are behind in their vocabulary and math. Frequently, they ask her to boost their grades up while she goes over their homework. Shaking her head, she answers, "I can't give you a higher grade. If you're willing to learn, I will teach you and you will improve."

Still, Luom makes them pay .50 cac, (about .01 cents) for each tutoring session. They are all happy, the students, the teachers, and even the principal.

Without her teacher, even a student as good as Luom is still a teenager. According to old Vietnamese people, a teenager is a devil. The fun begins for Luom when the classroom becomes her stage. Often, she stands up and makes everyone listen to her sing. Her voice fills up the classroom and goes into the next, easily passing through the one-foot opening at the top of the dividing wall. The boys from the next room listen, clapping their hands and laughing.

Two students banter back and forth until one of the boys on the other side takes a broomstick and throws it over the dividing wall. Luom orders some students to throw it back. They all take turns until finally it is Luom's turn to throw the broomstick. It does not go smoothly. She tosses the broomstick over and it lands directly on the forehead of the principal, who decided to come see what all the commotion is about.

Suddenly, the boy's classroom goes silent. Unaware of the situation on the other side, the girls still feel aggressive, especially Luom. They taunt the boys with name-calling and chicken noises. Though the boys do not respond at the command of the principal, they cannot hold in their laughter which erupts in little crackles. Over on Luom's side, the girls believe the boys are enjoying their humor. Meanwhile, the principal quietly enters the front of the girls' classroom.

Luom has her back to the entrance and is unaware of the principal standing behind her. Curious as to the sudden silence of the girls and their frozen postures, she turns around, only to bump directly into the principal. Luom quickly and nonchalantly turns back to the class. In her loud voice, shouts like a commander to her soldiers, "Attention!"

The principal and teachers always enjoy Luom's play-acting. The principal holds back a laugh as he asks with barely controlled emotions, "Who threw the broomstick?"

The silence becomes oppressive, but no one is willing to point the finger at Luom. Finally, the principal says, "If you won't tell me who did this, I'll make you girls stand here until you do."

Thoughts rush through Luom's mind. If she lets her friends stand like this, she will feel guilty the rest of her life and they will no longer respect her. Leadership is important to her. Luom turns slowly to the principal and admits, "Principal, sir, I'm the one who threw it, sir."

Standing straight, Luom's face is the face of a soldier. To the girls in the room, Luom is hilarious and they try hard not to let their chuckling escape.

The principal enjoys Luom's entertainment and it is hard for him to get upset. In a very low voice, he says, "*You* threw it onto my forehead?"

Luom bows her head waiting for punishment. Still looking at her, the principal tells Luom to dismiss the students for their break. Luom is to remain in the classroom. Once all of the students have left, the principal reaches into his wallet, takes out some money and asks her to go buy two ice creams for him. Luom leaves, pays for the ice cream and brings it back. She thinks the principal purchased one for a teacher; he takes one for himself and gives her the other.

She walks over and sits at the front of her classroom. The principal, following her, does the same. Luom is astonished at the way her principal is disciplining her. She knows the adults run the school just like one big happy family. The principal is more of a father figure to her and the teachers are more like mothers. She sits there with her thoughts, enjoying her ice cream in the company of the principal, even though they do not speak the entire time. They simply watch the students play.

A few minutes later, all the teachers get tired of waiting for the principal to return. They come into the classroom and see the pair sitting at the front the smacking of their lips over the tasty ice cream. One teacher pulls money from her pocket and asks Luom to run over to the ice cream cart so that they may all enjoy the ice cream together. Though the other students outside know what's happening, they do not mind that Luom is closer to the teachers.

Four hours of school goes smoothly every day for Luom. Most importantly, it is fun, which helps her escape stressful financial problems at home. To help her family, Luom takes in extra laundry from her mother's friend, Mrs. Huong, who works at the American base washing uniforms for the GIs. Luckily, Luom is able to make more money this way. She writes a letter asking Ut Thom to come help her with the business too.

Luom is able to put more food on the table and Ut Thom even refuses her pay. As a reward for their hard work, Luom takes out some money every week to rents book for both to read.

Unfortunately, Mrs. Danh disapproves of Luom continuing with school and reading, so she often makes it difficult. In spite of her mother's ridiculous thinking, Luom continues to rent books. Every night, Luom and her aunt cover themselves with the blanket to read.

Ut Thom sits up under the blanket to give it a tent-like shape and keep the blanket from burning. Meanwhile, Luom reads in a voice just loud enough for her aunt to hear.

If Mrs. Danh happens to notice, she threatens to take Luom's books away. It is hard to prevent giggling at a funny story. When Mrs. Danh hears, she is even more upset. Though curses and threats are directed at Luom, Mrs. Danh never takes the book away from her. Luom understands Mrs. Danh is angry because her husband never comes home and so she takes her anger out on her oldest daughter. Deep down, her love for her child is great. Mrs. Danh has never set foot in a school, and so, unable to read or write, she is incapable of understanding the importance of knowledge through reading. All she knows is how to be a mother and a good wife. Yet her husband is always looking for the better woman.

By now, Mr. Bay has been gone for a while, and has even stopped sending money to his family. To earn extra money, Mrs. Danh rents the front room to two local cops. One of them is Mr. Bay's former soldier.

One day while Luom is doing the laundry, she sees her principal approaching her house. He is actually coming to visit Luom's boss, Mrs. Huong. Immediately Luom stands up and bows to him.

Later on, Mrs. Huong comes over and says to her, "Luom, your principal asked me if you are a maid in this big home."

"What did you tell him?"

"I said, 'No, this is her parents' house.'"

"What was his reaction?"

"Well, he was stunned because you told him your father is a motorcycle driver."

"That was before, when we first came here from Sai Gon."

Mrs. Huong continues, "Your principal was admiring how humble your behavior is even though you're a rich kid. He likes your work—he and the teachers are proud to have you as a student."

After that, Mrs. Huong and Luom chitchat some more about the laundry business, and Luom smiles happily.

Remembering her past, she recalls how Mr. Bay started as a motorcycle driver while they lived in the Cao Dai compound and were quite poor. Back then, she had only three pairs of clothes for the whole week, two for school and one for home. Old and black with patches from bicycle wear, her pants were not pretty. Yet for the blouses, she did her best to keep them white.

Luom would rather dress that way than in fancy clothes. She has difficulty telling people who she is because of her father's unpredictable character. His appearance repeatedly changes. One minute Mr. Bay is someone very important, and the next, a ragged man. Luom is so confused about her father's identity that if someone asked about him, it was easier for her to say, "My father is a motorcycle driver for a living." The family might be living in a big home, but since her father has not sent money for quite some time, they are broke. Now the big home is just for looks.

Despite their financial hardships, Thu Huong, Diep, and Luom are the best students of that year. The State of Soc Trang rewards them with a whole year's supply of school materials. When Mrs. Danh hears the news, she is overwhelmed by her children's achievement. However, she thinks all those school supplies are too much for them alone. She decides to take some of the materials to her nieces and nephews on her husband's side, hoping that perhaps the gesture could bring him back to her.

Luom watches as Mrs. Danh quickly reduces her supply of school materials. Luom realizes she must come up with an idea quickly before they all disappear. After thinking it through carefully, she makes a bookshelf and mounts it high up on the wall. Since there is no ladder to climb up to it, the only the person who can access it is Luom.

The following day, when Mrs. Danh spots the shelf, she orders her daughter, "Luom, take the bookshelf down and give me some paper."

Luom shakes her head and firmly says to her mother, "No, Nanny! It is almost gone and we don't have enough for the whole year anymore."

Mrs. Danh is irritable, smiling at the same time as she threatens, "I'm going to whip your bottom."

Next, she turns to Thu Huong. "Thu Huong, climb up there and get it for me."

Thu Huong also shakes her head, refusing to do so. Mrs. Danh asks, "Who is your mother?"

Thu Huong points her finger at Mrs. Danh and says, "You're my mother."

"Then why don't you listen to me? Do what I ask. Aren't you worried that I'll be mad?"

Luom would never hurt her siblings, but the gleam in her eye as she locked gazes with Thu Huong was enough to take care of the situation. Thu Huong says to her mother, "Nanny, sister's face is more frightening than yours."

Flustered, Mrs. Danh turns finally to her son Diep, who is nowhere to be found. He refuses to be in the middle of this and left when she was not looking. Frustrated that all of her children are turning against her, Mrs. Danh goes to see Mrs. Huong to cool down.

It is lucky for Luom that Mrs. Danh gave away only notepads and did not take any important textbooks. Because of this, Luom is able to prepare for the high school state test, a tough obstacle to her continuing education. The state will take only the top two hundred fifty boys out of two thousand five hundred boys and the top two hundred girls out of two thousand. Luom is worried that if she is unable to pass, her school year will be over, since there is no way her parents could afford to pay for further education. She remembers so many girls, who had to quit school after sixth grade, stay home and wait until they turned sixteen to get married.

With this thought in mind, Luom awakens every morning at 4 am to study. She soon notices a white cat that appears in the house in these early mornings. She walks around to check for a hole somewhere, but the doors are closed and the walls are sealed. It seems inexplicable. Where is the white cat coming from? Going back to study, she frowns at it.

The cat meows and, coming close to Luom, allows her to stroke its fluffy fur. Its beauty astonishes her, having only envisioned a creature like this in stories. While petting the cat, Luom feels a mixture of emotion. She whispers into its ear, "I really don't want you to get shot like Kiki. I don't want anything to happen to you—I'm a jinx."

Before returning to her studies, Luom prays to God, her grandfather Mr. Ngoc, Tam Choi, her eight aunts and her little brother Hoang Huy. On the second night, again, the cat reappears and Luom spends half an hour playing with it. On the third night, exhausted from work, school and study, Luom oversleeps. She wakes up to the cat licking her face, as it was somehow able to get past her mosquito net. Lying there, Luom again wonders, how could the cat get in?

She walks around the house searching for any open area, but again, she can't find anything. After all, she closes everything up herself, every night. Luom's thoughts wander and suddenly, she thinks perhaps the cat is her aunt's spirit, come back to help her with her studies. Tam Choi was born in the year of the cat, and a white cat would make sense for Tam Choi, since she was kindhearted and tender. Luom cannot recall a single bad memory of her dead aunt. In that moment, Luom remembers that her mother dreamed of a visit from a white cat. The morning after, Mrs. Danh received news from home saying Tam Choi died in a Viet Cong attack. A grenade had exploded in front of the underground shelter where Tam Choi and two boys were trying to enter. Tam Choi and one of the boys died instantly. The other boy lost an eye.

The thought of the cat as her aunt's spirit grows stronger in Luom's mind with every passing moment. Chills run down her spine, and fear creeps into her head. She wants to pet the cat, but her hand shakes as she strokes the fur, her heart thumping rapidly in her chest. She enjoys being with it, but at the same time she is afraid of her aunt's ghost. In a fearful voice, Luom tells the cat, "Aunt Tam Choi, I love you, but if we keep going on like this, I'll not be able to study. I'll fail the test!"

The cat seems to understand Luom; it licks her hand and face for a long time, and then disappears into the still-dark morning. Luom begins her studies again. A few weeks later, weary from work and study, she wake up late. Mysteriously, the cat reappears in her bed and lies patiently beside her. As Luom turns her body, she feels the soft fur in her arms and it helps her to slowly open her sleepy eyes. When her vision comes into focus, Luom sees the cat good-naturedly stretched across the table and she walks over to begin her studies. It watches without a sound.

The morning of her test, Luom gets up at two o'clock in the morning. By six o'clock, she has prepared breakfast and is ready to go to school for her test. The cat is nowhere in sight.

Chapter 23
Struggle

Luom sets foot on the high school grounds for the first time. It is the biggest school in the state of Soc Trang, and she feels lost almost immediately. Standing there amongst the masses of students, her eyes search for any sign of a familiar face. Unfortunately, the teachers split all the students apart. Looking up, Luom scans the list of names on the bulletin board that says where she is supposed to go. The noise from the surrounding students is hard to ignore and Luom begins to wish she was elsewhere until she spots her name. Seeing it there in print triggers her sense of determination and with a renewed energy, she heads off toward her assigned room.

Taking her seat, Luom envisions her principal. She remembers the confidence in his eyes, and the memory slowly seeps into her as the exam begins.

The first subject is math followed by an essay, and Luom flies easily through both of them. Next comes history. Here, she hits her first obstacle. There are two questions on Cambodia, one about how big the country is and the other about its population. Staring at the questions on the page, Luom realizes she simply does not know the answer. Briefly considering why this is the case, she suddenly remembers. The section on Cambodia in Luom's history book had served as a replacement when Mrs. Danh ran out of toilet paper. When Cambodia came up in class, Luom bowed her head, embarrassed and silent at her mother's use of the history book.

After the exam, on her way home, Luom dwells on the questions she was unable to answer, thinking about what they might mean for her future. She feels like a failure and worries that she will be unable to continue school. Her stomach is so tied up in knots that she cannot even share her feelings with anyone. Anyway, she is used to keeping things to herself.

A week later, the results of the exam are posted on the wall of the school. If she did not pass, which in her mind feels rather likely, she will not only be embarrassed for herself, but will also bring shame to her parents.

Luom walks to the school, feeling smaller and smaller as she nears the paper plastered to the wall. Luckily, there is no one there to recognize her. Peering out from under her coconut hat, she looks for her name. Luom's eyes widen. Not only has she passed, she earned a very high score.

On the way home, Luom feels good inside, and under the shade of the coconut hat, she smiles to herself. She wants to jump, she wants to scream, but she knows that in public, as a respectable girl, she cannot give the impression of being either happy or sad. Therefore, she walks home much the same as always. Looking ahead and following a straight path, she walks just the way her grandmother, Mrs. Ho Thiet, had taught her—with no glance to either side.

Quoi, the man renting the room in her house, waits for her at the front door. He asks directly, "Did you pass?"

Luom manages to crack a tiny smile in his direction, but is too worried someone will see her beside Quoi to stop and talk. Especially with a man, it would be considered flirting.

Passing without a word to Quoi, she approaches her mother lying in the hammock. "Nanny, I passed."

On the hammock, Mrs. Danh remains facing the wall, unmoved by Luom's achievement. Well! Luom did not expect anything different. Her mother always seals her emotions inside the way she was taught as a child.

Not bothered by her mother's silence, Luom goes back to work. She has three months to plan her high school year and the anticipation makes Luom happier than ever. She still worries about money: how she will afford things she needs; the white *Ao Dai*; the books…

Luom shares none of her troubles with anyone, but luckily, Quoi asks Mrs. Danh to let Luom wash his clothes and cook for him. Luom is enthusiastic at the prospect of earning some extra money. Her mother agrees only to the washing. While Mr. Bay is absent, cooking for another man is unacceptable in the public eye.

Although Mrs. Danh outwardly shows no sign of caring about her daughter's achievement, she plans to somehow let her husband know about Luom's accomplishment. After all, Mrs. Danh understands Luom will need money for the *Ao Dai* outfit. She sends a letter the next day. Not much later she receives one from Mr. Bay, with money enclosed and a note promising to return home soon.

Mrs. Danh takes Luom to the store every day for a week, shopping for material to make the *Ao Dai*. She has difficulty choosing the right tailor but finally finds one from far away with many years of experience. The woman fits Luom and gives her elegant high heeled shoes that make Luom walk differently.

Three summer months pass quickly, and Luom begins school. The first day she feels uncomfortable in her new outfit and shoes. Though she wore them when chanting, now she notices people looking at her, whispering behind her back. Some of the boys said, "Look at those peaches."

Others said, "Those oranges."

Luom tries to ignore them, but the more she tries, the more stiffly she walks.[5]

Mrs. Danh is stunned at how well her daughter looks in the outfit, and hopes her husband will soon be home to see his daughter all grown up.

After many months absence, Mr. Bay finally comes home with good news. He is now a Major in the Army. He is even happier knowing his daughter passed the high school exam. He asks Luom, "What second language did you choose?"

"Major Sir, I chose French."

Considering for a moment, Major Bay takes a fountain pen from his pocket, hands it to Luom and says, "I hope this will help you. I think you should switch to English, though. It would be useful, and

---

5   Ao Dai is a long dress. High school girls have to wear white Ao Dai like uniform.

will take you even further in life."

Luom's eyes glow brightly when she sees the pen her father has just handed to her. Owning this fountain pen is like a teenager in America owning a car. Nodding her head enthusiastically, Luom answers her father, "Yes! I'll do that tomorrow Major."

Standing nearby, Quoi overhears the conversation between father and daughter. He buys Luom an English dictionary. After school, as Luom walks home, Quoi waits in the front room, dictionary in hand. When she enters the door, he gives it to her and Luom looks up at him gratefully. Opening the dictionary to explore its pages, Luom immediately sees a letter inside. She reads it slowly. In it, Quoi expresses his feelings for her and asks if she feels any passion for him. Meanwhile, Quoi stands by awaiting her reaction.

Luom smiles and walks away.

Luom is excited to continue her education and even better, her parents don't have to pay for it. Also happy with the two gifts from her father and Quoi, she is busy planning her coming school year. High school is filled with many things to learn and many people to meet.

Luom is quickly fascinated with the English language and comes to admire her two teachers greatly. One of them, Mrs. Ngoc Lan, always dresses in beautifully colored *Ao Dai* and high heeled shoes. She walks with music flowing from her footsteps, almost dancing to her own tune. Luom's other teacher is American. Tall and handsome, he teaches half an hour of conversational English following Mrs. Ngoc Lan's teachings of the meaning of the words. The pair is incomparable. Luom often closes her eyes to picture herself as Mrs. Ngoc Lan.

With all the wonders that Luom's future promises, she completely forgets about Quoi, waiting for her to answer his letter. A week goes by, a month goes by, and soon Quoi becomes frustrated with her silence.

Quoi is unwilling to forget Luom that easily; he tries to win her. One day, looking through his window, he sees a young teacher from the neighborhood. Her feet are stuck in the muddy road. Quoi asks Luom, "Luom, could I go out to help the teacher with her suitcase?"

For some reason, Luom is upset and says dismissively, "Do what you want. Stop asking questions, don't bother me."

Quoi smiles and again, he asks, "Could you loan me the

dictionary?"

Luom takes the book and tosses it on his bed. Later that day, Quoi gives the book back to her. Again, there is a letter inside. This time it contains a proposal of marriage for when Luom finishes school. Quoi finally gets her attention, and his charm and romantic letter allure her. However, Luom wants Quoi to stop bothering her, so she writes to him, "Yes, I'll marry you when I get out, when I'm done with what I'm doing. Now please leave me alone with my school."

Quoi is happy with this answer. Every week from that day, Luom receives a letter from him, always planning for their future together.

Daily at noon after school, while Luom does the laundry, Quoi takes a chair and sits behind her, listening as she sings. Uncomfortable with what could easily turn into neighborhood gossip, Luom gives him an unfriendly look and forbids him to come any closer. After all, their relationship is unacceptable. Quoi is older than Luom by seven years, and he hasn't yet asked her parents for permission.

One dark night, Quoi waits for Luom to go outside, and then grabs hold of her hand and plants a kiss on her cheek. Startled, Luom pushes him away, her body trembling from fright. All night long, she is unable to sleep.

The following morning, Luom turns all of Quoi's letters over to her mother. She cannot erase the worry that Quoi might attempt more than a kiss and do something that she is unable to avoid. Mrs. Danh is mainly annoyed with the news, hoping Quoi would marry her sister Ut Thom, not her daughter. She does not understand why Luom showed her the letters or what Luom is trying to prevent. Nonetheless, Mrs. Danh asks Quoi to move out, with the promise he may visit every two weeks.

Luom is finally at peace for a few days. Then comes Ngoc Nhung, the girl next door, to chitchat with Luom. Her eyes open wide when Ngoc Nhung tells Luom she thinks she is pregnant. Luom, matching her friend's expression, asks, "How did you become pregnant?"

"I sat next to that man across from your house."

"You mean....that handsome guy?"

"Yes!"

Luom looks off, wondering aloud. "How did he get so

handsome anyway?"

"People say he is half Chinese and half Cambodian."

"Hmmm." Luom turns again to Ngoc Nhung. "But he is married."

"Yes, he is married."

"When did you sit next to him?"

"Yesterday."

"Oh." Luom though about this a second, then exclaimed, "Oh my God! Quoi tried to kiss me."

"What did you do?"

"I pushed him away! But how can I tell if I am pregnant?"

Suddenly assuming an air of command, Ngoc Nhung orders Luom, "Put your finger on your throat and feel your pulse. If it is jumping fast that means you're pregnant."

Both girls slowly reach up to their necks and place their index fingers on the side. Luom is first to break the silence. "I don't feel anything."

Ngoc Nhung whispers, her voice trembling, "Push harder."

Another moment of scared silence, then Luom screams in a strangled whisper, "Oh my God! I'm pregnant!"

Ngoc Nhung says knowingly, "I know, you have to be."

"How did you know?" Luom turns her fearful face to her friend.

"Because you told me he tried to kiss you."

"And you? Are you pregnant too?"

Ngoc Nhung presses her finger into her throat again, harder this time, and quickly turns to Luom. Her expression is unmistakable. "I'm pregnant too!"

Chapter 24
Dim-witted

As usual every afternoon, Luom does laundry for Mrs. Huong. While she goes through the pocket of the GI's uniform, she finds a condom inside. Ut Thom and Luom are excited; they thought they had found a balloon to play with, not realizing its true function. Using all their breath, they try to puff it up, but are unsuccessful. Luom and Ut Thom run to Mrs. Danh asking for her help. "Nanny, can you help us blow this up?"

Mrs. Danh also tries, without success. She concludes, "It must be a water balloon. Put in some water."

Luom happily runs to try it out and in no time, Ut Thom and Luom are playing with their very own water balloon. They dangle it up and down, flipping it from side to side, tossing and catching. At that moment, Major Bay happens to walk in and sees it swaying from Luom's hand. Surprised, and then upset, he orders Luom, "Luom, bring it over here."

But Luom is reluctant to give it up. "Major, it's just a water balloon, please let me play with it."

Major Bay, unable to explain things of this nature to his daughter, grinds his teeth in frustration. "I know it's a water balloon, but you are too big to play like a child. Give it to me."

Luom refuses to succumb so easily and tries instead to convince her father to let her keep it. "But Major Sir, look! It's shaped unusually too. It looks like a sausage."

Now Major Bay is annoyed, yet he can't help but burst out laughing, happy to knowing Luom is still innocent. Ut Thom, Luom and all her siblings gaze at Major Bay, wondering what he will do next. It is not often that Major Bay becomes so upset over something as simple as child's play. Mrs. Danh, hoping to fix the situation, whispers to her husband, "*Minh Oi*! It's just a water balloon, let her have some fun."

Irritated with his wife, Major Bay pulls her into the bedroom to explain. A few minutes later, they come out and Mrs. Danh says to Luom with a giggle, "Luom give it to your father. I'll explain later."

Major Bay takes the condom, dumps out all the water, stuffs it in his pocket and walks out of the house. None of them understands why he is so upset. Meanwhile, Quoi comes for a visit. Hidden from sight during the argument, Quoi appears as Major Bay fades into the distance. He heard everything. Furtively flashing his eyes at Luom, he says with a mocking laugh, "Water balloon."

Luom glares at him. Still confused about why her father took away her fun, she does not take kindly to Quoi's teasing. Her anger quickly boils up. Snatching up all the shoes around the house, she pitches them at Quoi, sometimes missing him and other times hitting him squarely on the back. Ut Thom and Luom's siblings, too, are disgusted with Quoi's actions and add to the frenzy by suggesting that she drown him in the pond.

But Quoi only laughs harder. "Yes! Go ahead, drown me in the pond. We'll see which one of us will sink."

Luom rounds on him, another shoe held menacingly above her head, and orders Quoi out. "Go. Away!"

Quoi calls out for help to Mrs. Danh, who drags her sister close and whispers something in her ear. Ut Thom's face is flushed as she walks up to Luom. "Give it up, I'll tell you."

Luom drops the shoe and follows her aunt outside. Ut Thom faces Luom and says matter-of-factly, "That is the thing people put the baby into."

Remembering her humiliation, Luom feels a fresh sense of anger at her lack of knowledge about sex. Voicing her frustration, she asks her aunt, "Why didn't anybody explain it to me the way you just told me? Why do they have to make it a big deal and be so secretive?"

She pauses a moment, looking at her aunt, then a slight frown spreads across her forehead. "But…that thing is too small to put the baby in."

Ut Thom smiles and says over her shoulder as she walks through the door, "You'll understand later." Luom shakes her head, still doubting her answer, and follows her aunt inside.

Quoi asks Luom, "So you understand it now?"

Feeling more confident, Luom answers defiantly, "Yes! That's the thing they put the baby inside."

Quoi, again mocking her, whispers, "How are we going to get married if you don't even know what it is? I'll teach you later."

Luom is even more angry with Quoi. "No you won't."

"Then who will?"

Luom avoids his eyes and walks away. At least the afternoon had ended with a little laughter for the family, something not heard in their house for long time. Even Mrs. Danh found a little fun in it.

Chapter 25
Disappointment's Journey

Again, Major Bay leaves, unaware his wife is pregnant. A few months later, Mrs. Danh asks Luom to go visit her father. It takes her all day on the bus to get to her destination. Ca Mau is the city where Major Bay is stationed, and where Major Bay's younger brother has a second house. The other house is in the same city where Luom lives. Major Bay manages to take his mother and his younger brother with him wherever he goes.

When Luom arrives, Mrs. Ho Thiet is downhearted to see her granddaughter. No one else is happy to see her, either. Major Bay asks his daughter, "Why are you here?"

Luom looks up at her father. "Major, I came to visit you."

In a low voice, Major Bay says to her, "You're growing up and I don't want you to visit me anymore. This visit should be your last."

His voice is low and soft, but the words stab Luom through the heart. Unwilling to let the hurt show in her face, she barely controls her tears. Looking straight into her father's eyes, Luom levels her voice and says, "Yes, Father, I understand and this will be my last visit."

The rest of her family looks at her with pity. Major Bay gently places money on the table for the bus ride home. To Luom it is a slap in the face.

She quietly accepts the money. Even though her emotions are building, she still manages to gaze into the faces of everyone watching.

She wants to remember this moment forever as a reminder to herself. She tells herself if she ever gets married she'll find a good man, and not ever settle for less. Luom tries to reconcile the love she had for her father with the emptiness she feels looking at the man before her. She had always loved her father; she admired him in so many ways for so many years. But today's darkness came from her father's soul alone.

It seems that in every face, from young to old, she sees an evil that has taken their soul. Luom wonders, has she entered hell? They all shift uneasily beneath her grim gaze. Finally, Luom turns around to face Ba Tam Chi, the woman whom her father calls a childhood friend, the woman who is supposed to be her mother's friend. Ba Tam Chi's oldest daughter is the same age as Luom, sitting on the hammock beside Major Bay. Her mind fills with questions. What is going on? she wonders. Why are they here? She begins to reorder her thoughts, trying to understand why her father treats her this way.

Mrs. Ho Thiet sees Luom's face covered in disappointment, or perhaps something more than that. However, the only thing she cares about in that moment is to find a quick solution for everyone. Pointing to Ba Tam Chi, she tells her granddaughter, "Luom, this is your second mother. Go over and say hello."

Staring at her grandmother, Luom says resolutely, "Ba Noi, I have only one mother, though your superstitions forbid me to call her so. This woman is supposed to be my parents' best friend. I'll not obey you, Ba Noi."

Furiously, Major Bay smacks his hand down on the table and points his finger at Luom. "Get out of my sight!"

Mrs. Ho Thiet pulls her granddaughter toward her and whispers, "Luom, make your father happy and he'll reward you."

Luom glances at her grandmother and says, "What reward? The reward of taking care of his children and his worn-out wife after he's used us all up?"

The remark hangs in the air as everyone stares in shock. Even Luom cannot believe what had come from her own mouth. Major Bay's face reddens in humiliation at Luom's words. Awkward silence continues for a moment until as if, on cue, everyone resumes their tasks, ignoring Luom entirely. They finish preparing the food, neglecting to offer her any, as they gather to eat as one, big, cheerful family. It is clear—Luom is not welcome.

The smell of food rises through the air, a mixture of smells from the various dishes on the table. All she can think of is home, where they try to survive, and here, where her father and his family stuff their faces with food. The hunger begins to gnaw at the inside of Luom's stomach. To take her mind off her hunger, she walks out to the street, next to the river bank that is called Kinh 16. The surroundings seem familiar at first, and then Luom remembers. This is where Luom's parent's house was a long time ago. The place Major Bay used to digs his hands down into the mud hole to find eels for food for the family.

It is not long before the mosquitoes swarm. Their cacophonous buzzing fills her ears. They enjoy their meal as Luom is left without hers.

Finally, unable to continue the losing battle against the mosquitoes, she enters the house quietly. Unnoticed, Luom finds a corner of the front room where she can lie down. With no blanket or pillow, only a thin layer of dust covering the floor, the night seems longer than ever. Luom tosses and turns restlessly, her hand slapping at the ever-present mosquitoes. Finally, through her half-slumber she hears the chickens *coo, coo, coo,* letting her know it is 3 a.m. It is still very early, but she doesn't want to stay longer than she must. The early bus leaves at 6 a.m. She washes her face quietly, and slips swiftly out of the door.

Chapter 26
The Hunters

Luom feels breathless as she walks to the bus station. A chill reaches through to her very bones, and her sweat makes her even colder. At one point, dizziness forces her to rest at the side of the road. This happened to her once before at her Grandmother Duong's house. While everyone was joyfully celebrating the New Year, Luom lay in bed. As the pain and confusion slowly ease off, Luom is able to continue to the bus station. She finds a seat near the window and for a long time barely moves, letting her mind wander.

Luom does not realize where the bus stopped: in her mother's hometown, next to the market her cousin Bia owns. From a distance, she hears someone calling to her, "Hey! Luom! Are you going to say hello?"

Bia's voice brings Luom back into the real world. She exits the bus and walks like a zombie into Bia's house. Bia starts to gather some fruits from her basket and hands them to her cousin. Luom asks her, "Have you sold any?"

"Yes, I made some money, don't you worry."

Ba Vit, Bia's father, walks in. Luom bows her head in greeting to her uncle and his wife Mo Ba. Mo Ba reaches deep into her pocket, bringing out some money she hands to Luom. Luom graciously accepts it and again bows to say thank you. When Ba Vit sees his niece's tears, he tries to reassure her and smiles. "We are your family; don't worry about paying it back."

Bia tells her father, "I'm going to grandmother's house with Luom."

Luom and Bia leave the market, making their way to Grandmother Duong. On the way, Bia tries to find the answer to Luom's sadness. She asks her cousin, "Why are you so gloomy? Some city boy broke your heart?"

Luom lies, "Yes! Those young city boys are rotten."

Bia asks, "Well, why don't you like country boys? They're very good people. You get married and that's it."

Her thoughts shortly distracted, Luom smiles at Bia and thinks, "Yes! Country boys just like my father."

Along the way, Luom's sixth uncle, Sau Guong and his wife, Mo Sau, spot Luom and Bia walking together. They call to Luom, "Come here! We have something for you."

Luom and Bia walk into Sau Guong's house, and Mo Sau hands some money to Luom. She accepts it without hesitation. She is grateful for her mother's family. Normally only Mrs. Duong solved Luom's problems. This time the whole family is helping. They know what Luom's mother is going through and her daughter does not need to ask for anything.

Thanking her uncle and his wife, the pair heads toward Grandmother Duong's house. Mrs. Duong had been preparing food, planning a visit to see her pregnant daughter, but Luom beats her to it.

The dried fish, rice, fruits, vegetables, and now some money, all this could take care of Luom's family for quite some time. She stays overnight at her grandmother's house.

The quiet days in the rice paddy countryside are cheerful, especially when visitors surprise the family and all gather to exchange stories. Bay Thoi appears at the door step. He opens his wallet and hands Luom half of his salary for that month. Luom gazes at her uncle. As he gazes back, she knows he understands her concern. How will he be able to survive with so little until next month? Already she knows that he lives paycheck to paycheck. At least he does not have to support a family of his own yet, for Bay Thoi tends to think of money only one day to the next.

Still, looking at Luom, he reassures her. "Don't worry, it will be fine."

Visiting Mr. and Mrs. Duong is the most rewarding for Luom. She waits as her grandfather, Mr. Duong, tries to catch a chicken for the special meal celebrating the return of his granddaughter and his son. It is not long before they catch and cook the chicken into a delicious soup. Luom feels the steam rising past her nose, bringing thoughts of her mother and siblings. They are not here to enjoy this delicious meal and it is too expensive to have chickens back home. They have chicken only once a year on the anniversary of Grandfather Ngoc's death. Silent tears begin to roll down her face as her emotions build. She tries to wipe them away unseen. Before she can dry her cheeks, Mr. Duong, noticing Luom's grief, says aloud to Mrs. Duong, "We should send our daughter a chicken."

"Yes! We should."

A loud commotion babbles up from the children around the table. "And a duck, too!"

Luom loses her downcast gaze and her lips crack into a tiny smile. She can bring a whole chicken and duck home! All the children race to the barn clamoring to help Luom first.

"Luom, which one do you want?"

A bright smile now on her face, Luom points her finger to the biggest chicken and duck. "Those two."

"Quick, give her some eggs!"

"Better not take all the eggs!"

"But Grandmother doesn't mind how much we give her. She always says Luom's family needs food more than us. Besides, they will lay more eggs."

All the children are taught to share throughout childhood, especially with Luom's family, since Mrs. Danh lives so far away.

The sky slowly starts to darken. Night falls. Mr. Duong lights up an oil lamp, which spreads a warm glow around the room. The night creatures crawl out from under the cover of darkness and lend their sounds to the nightly concert. The family is shielded in a bubble of light from the chilling blackness of the countryside. The family cemetery sits just behind the house.

The house fills with voices and laughter until Mrs. Duong says in a harsh whisper, "Quiet, listen."

Dogs can be heard from far up the road, barking and pulling

at chains. Mr. and Mrs. Duong's dog, ears pricked, joins the chorus of barks and howls.

Mrs. Duong leans over the table and blows out the oil lamp. Looking through the hole in the coconut wall, she sees three dark shadows approaching her house under the crescent moon's light. She turns around quickly and lays an index finger to her lips for everyone to keep quiet.

Wrapping Luom and Bay Thoi into her arms, she walks them to the bedroom and hastily pushes them in. Telling them to stand aside, she flips up the bamboo mat on the floor. Beneath are two cement pots that Luom's father made long ago. She motions for both to go in and as they reach the floor, Luom sees a small tunnel that leads to the cemetery. Darkness shrouds their path. Too terrified to go forward, the pair remain at the entrance.

In the house, the family can feel the night surround them and close in. Ut Thom and Bia crawl into bed, pretending to be asleep. Suddenly, loud knocks rap on the door. A voice from outside says loudly, *"Day la Anh em Bo Doi, giai phong mien nam."* (This is the South Vietnam rescue mission brothers.)

Mr. Duong waits to reply for a moment, then he says in a falsely sleepy voice, "Who?"

Ignoring him, they demand, "Open the door."

Mr. Duong's mouth opens wide and a loud yawn escapes it as he unhurriedly goes to light up the oil lamp. Once finished, he unties the rope and lifts up the wooden stick lying across the door. Staring out with sleepy eyes, he complains, "What is so important that you people cannot wait until tomorrow morning?"

Like three shadows, the men dressed in black come into view. Without hesitation, one of them asks, "Where is the daughter of the former Police Chief? And where is your son?"

Mr. Duong lies easily, "Both left earlier. Why do you want my granddaughter and my son?"

"The Police Chief's daughter is a clever young lady. We remember when she was young. Your son must work as a double agent for us. But you should not worry."

"That's impossible, my granddaughter is still a child and you are asking her to go against her father."

"That girl isn't a child anymore; she is a bright young woman."

Without invitation, the group of men enters the house and begins their search for Luom and Bay Thoi. Ut Thom and Bia remain lying on top of the bamboo mat, still pretending sleep as they conceal Luom and their brother beneath. One man turns to Mrs. Duong, "You must go with us. We'll hold you hostage until they come to make an exchange."

Mr. Duong says to the men, "Let me go instead."

"No. No one will take us seriously if we take you hostage. It must be your wife."

"Do not harm my wife, I will never forgive you," Mr. Duong tells them, looking straight into their eyes. "Wait here; let me go get a sweater for her."

"Of course."

Quickly, Mr. Duong grabs a sweater and puts it around his wife's shoulders. Mrs. Duong's eyes signal to her husband not to worry and she quietly walks out with the men.

Luom and Bay Thoi hear the sound of Mr. Duong closing the door, but to make sure, they wait until Ut Thom removes the mat. Mr. Duong says quietly, "You both have to leave by morning."

Luom answers, "Yes! Ong Ngoai. But what are we going to do about Ba Ngoai?"

"Don't be troubled about her. She is a strong woman. She will turn the situation around and come home to us. They will not harm her."

Bay Thoi feels tormented inside. He is a soldier from the South, but the Viet Cong want him to be their secret agent, and he knows he must make a deal for his mother to return home. The more difficult circumstance is that Mr. Duong's side of the family is Viet Cong and the people who took his wife hostage are members of his own family.

The night is long for everyone. Unable to sleep, all they can do is stare into the darkness. The house must remain dark and silent to avoid the unwanted attention that would soon turn into rumors. Vietnamese people always remind one another, "*Tai vach, mach rung.*" (The walls have ears and the jungle has veins.)

Outside, the night creatures again have their chance to perform. The chorus of their voices rises from the cemetery, a sound that plays with the fear and uncertainty in the house.

It's a long time before the chickens call, "*Coo, coo, coo, coo.*"

Mr. Duong rushes Ut Thom to cook some rice for breakfast. The family again gathers for the morning meal. Afterwards, Bay Thoi and Luom hop on the first bus out of the village. It is extremely dangerous for both to travel in the early hours, but necessary.

For security, a group of soldiers on their Jeep goes first. They come upon a pond of mud. The soldiers stop. Carefully, they search the area, find the booby traps and dismantle them, and pass through safely without casualties.

Though Luom often travels like this, she has been blessed with good fortune so far.

Chapter 27
On the Way Home

The bus passes through the village where Luom's father was once powerful and well respected. Luom knows it will go by her old house. Determined to find out where the hearts of Ba Di Nam's family lie, Luom tells Bay Thoi that she must make a visit to them. Bay Thoi agrees quietly and asks the bus driver to stop.

Ba Di Nam's family is surprised. After being invited in, Luom crosses the room, eyes intently focused on the pictures lining the wall. There is a picture of a little girl next to her own picture and the girl resembles her brother Si. Luom asks Tu Lua, Ba Di Nam's daughter, "Aunt Tu Lua, who is this little girl?"

The evidence is before Luom's eyes and Tu Lua is unable to remain silent. She answers, "She is your sister."

The truth hits Luom like a bus. She realizes her father is living with another family—his family but not hers. She turns around abruptly and walks out of their house. Tu Lua calls after her, "Luom! Luom, come back here, I want to explain."

"You don't need to, the picture says it all."

Standing at the road, Luom waits for the bus to bring her home. Tears again trail down her face. She is angry with herself and commands herself to stop crying. She knew what she would find before she even saw the picture.

Sitting on the bus, Luom is disgusted by what she's just learned. Her father and his family have misused Luom's mother and her siblings.

All of his actions are simply because the other woman has money to buy his love. Right and wrong no longer matter to them.

Luom's father wants to be a more powerful man through this woman. He can have a stronger connection to higher authority. Those like her mother, with no education, who work on the rice paddies, no longer fit in with Mr. Bay's everyday life. Tam Chi is her father's queen for now: rich, sharp, and willing to do anything to help Mr. Bay climb the ladder of success.

Luom mumbles, "I wish I never knew any of you."

The trip home finally ends. Getting off the bus, lost in sorrow, Luom walks home.

The sun reaches the horizon, but it is still bright enough outside for her to spot her old principal. He is Cambodian, a tall man with a dark complexion who always expressed concerned about Luom. She will never forget him. Wasting no time, she runs to catch up. Arriving before him, she circles her arms to her chest and bows.

"Hi, principal."

Not recognizing the teenager before him, he asks, "Who are you?"

"Luom, principal."

"Of course," he chuckles, "only you would run after me just to say hello." He inspects her a little more closely. "You're growing up! How is school?"

"I'm in high school now, and I'm doing great."

"You are in high school? I knew I was not wrong about you."

"What are you doing here, Principal?"

"I'm coming home for a visit to my family."

"You are from around here?"

"Soc Trang is in Cambodia, don't you know?" Smiling, he continues, "Keep it up, Luom, I often think about you."

"I'm trying. Thank you, principal."

Both say goodbye. The chance meeting is a twist of fate that gives Luom some cheerfulness. The five mile walk home no longer seems so far.

Since Luom left home, every day her siblings have waited for her on the bridge. Soon they see her silhouette from far away and the children shout, "Look! It looks like sister number two is coming home!"

"Yes, yes! That is her."

They run towards their sister, grab the bags she is carries, and bring them into the house. Luom's youngest brother jumps on the table, and starts to pick at the knots on the bags, trying to get the first look. The children are so happy to see Luom with food. They pry her with questions. "Food, food! All these came from father?"

Luom, to avoid disappointing her mother, whispers quietly, "They're from Ong, Ba Ngoai and all the family members."

Innocent of the reason for her whispering, one of the children pipes up, "Did you have fun while you were there?"

"Yes! I had a lot of fun."

Drawing near to Mrs. Danh's hammock, Luom says, "Nanny, I'm home."

Mrs. Danh's face stays turned to the wall as always. She does not even acknowledge her daughter's return. Yet, Luom knows her mother hears her, so she moves away and heads to the kitchen. As she puts things away, she is happy with the food and money everyone has given their family. It will last a while.

That evening, Luom cooks Bun Nuoc Leo, a fish soup that everyone favors. She makes a bowl for her mother and places it on the table next to the hammock. "Nanny, please get up and eat, I made your favorite."

Mrs. Danh stirs and rises to sit at the table. As she eats, she gazes at her children filling themselves hungrily. The eyes that stare out from her face are sad and reddened as if she has been crying. Yet she must laugh at the children's jokes and especially at the attempt of Dung and Si to enter the conversation, as they babble away in baby talk. Once in a while, Mrs. Danh turns her face to the wall, trying to shield her emotion. For Luom, she is simply happy that her mother got up to eat and talk to them.

Cheerfully, Luom says, "Nanny, is my soup good?"

Mrs. Danh smiles with her sad face. "It's delicious."

"But it's not like yours, Nanny. Is this your favorite dish?"

Mrs. Danh shakes her head. "This is your father's favorite. I cooked it so much since I married him, it became my specialty."

Mrs. Danh chokes on her words every time she talks about her husband. Again, she turns her face away to hide her tears. There is no way for Mrs. Danh to escape this marriage. Her parents obey Vietnamese tradition, and therefore, she must obey as well. The parents arrange the marriage and if it does not work out, she must cope with it on her own. There is no chance of a divorce. It would be shameful to her parents and to herself. There is a saying, *Chong chua, Vo toi.* It means the husband is king, and the wife, a slave. Men can have as many wives as they want while the women serve as one of their worn-out toys. Some men even brag about their ability to attract women and some bring home other women to the family. Yet there remain some faithful men. Major Bay is not one of them.

Mrs. Danh's heart is broken. Forbidden to show her jealousy, she must conceal the truth. While others may seek those women who steal their husbands in anger, Mrs. Danh hums poems to calm herself.

Surprisingly, their neighbors are unaware that Mrs. Danh and her children have been abandoned, even though the houses are packed close together. They simply think Major Bay is too busy doing his duty to return home. Whatever they notice about the family's situation, it is a way of life in Vietnam, and no one is really concerned.

Dung and Si, the babies of the family, repeat happily after their mother. "This is my specialty, too!"

The antics of the two boys temporarily break the sadness in the house. Again, her children's laughter bring Mrs. Danh back to the present.

Luom, looking at her older siblings, reminds them, "Remember to do your homework."

Si rubs in smartly, "Remember, we still have a chicken and a duck outside from our grandparents. You guys do your homework, we will cook it tomorrow and save some for you when you all get home from school. No homework, no chicken!"

Si is rather adorable and instead of feeling irritated, everyone laughs and teases him with their tongues sticking out. "No homework, no chicken!"

Mrs. Danh turns to Luom and asks her daughter, "Why are you always making them study?"

"They must do their homework, Nanny."

Mrs. Danh replies, "I get tired always hearing about school from you. School, school, school, day in and day out."

Chapter 28
Humiliation

Many of the women in Mrs. Danh's generation are unable to read and write, unless they come from a rich or educated family. In her generation and in generations past, most women just get married, staying barefoot and often pregnant.

Mrs. Danh's father, Mr. Duong, is well versed in Chinese Confucian writing and music; unfortunately, he is illiterate in the Vietnamese language. Mr. Duong often mentions the differences between written Chinese and Vietnamese confuse him; he becomes frustrated when he has to ask Luom or someone else to read for him. Some of his children are unable to go to school. But Luom saw the struggle and was determined to learn.

Financing the household is always a problem. It was hard for Luom to focus on her school work. She always tried her best.

She had an idea that might work. She suggests to her mother, "Nanny, we could open a coffee shop. We have a good location for it."

"No! Your father would be rejected."

"Why?"

Annoyed, Mrs. Danh answers, "Because he wouldn't want men hanging around here."

"Nanny, how are we going to survive?"

Mrs. Danh now sounds exhausted. "Well, do what you can, use your brain. What are you going to school for anyway?"

"How about growing vegetables? We still have some land beside the house. We could raise chickens, ducks and pigs."

"No, too much work."

"I'll take care of them."

Now thoroughly agitated with Luom's nagging and ideas, Mrs. Danh wants to end the conversation. "I said no! And I mean no. Don't ask me again."

Frowning in anger, Mrs. Danh turns on her heel and walks away. The truth is that Mrs. Danh wants Luom to quit school and take care of the family, but she is too afraid of her husband's reaction.

The relationship between Mrs. Danh and Luom is not a happy one. Mrs. Danh is greatly disturbed by Quoi's visits to Luom, even though she is the one who gave him permission. Each time Quoi leaves her house, Mrs. Danh grinds her teeth and says to Luom, "My sister should be the one to receive this proposal. It shouldn't be for you, you devil teen."

Luom could not care less who Quoi marries, as long as she does not become pregnant before the wedding. It is most important for Luom to continue her schooling. Nonetheless, she is hurt by her mother's words. Determined to hide her emotions, Luom focuses on her studies and taking care of the family. She understands it is not easy for Mrs. Danh to carry a child. This is her mother's fourteenth pregnancy, six children alive and seven dead. She has birthed so many children; there is no more energy for her to function. And she can no longer rely on her husband, who has abandoned his family to start a new one.

Luom looks in the rice container. It's empty. She says aloud to her mother, "Nanny, we have no more rice for tomorrow."

"Go to the house across the road and ask them if we can borrow some of their rice."

Luom grabs an empty condensed milk can and walks over to the neighbor. Mr. Tu and his family are dining. Bowing her head, Luom says, "Please, Mr. and Mrs. Tu, may I borrow a can of rice?"

Mr. Tu is a big man. Without his shirt, his belly hangs down over his pants. Some Vietnamese would say he is an *Ong Dia*, a Money Buddha who represents the richness of man, an image of what everyone would like to be. Glancing at Luom, Mr. Tu slowly picks up a piece of meat with his chopsticks and places it in his mouth. His jaws mash together as he grunts in pleasure. To Luom, the man looks like *Bac Giai*, a pig in human form, a friend of *Te Thien Dai Thanh* in the ancient Chinese story. He orders his wife, "Go in and get her a can of rice."

When his wife returns, she hands the rice to Luom. Mr. Tu picks up another piece of meat, his jaws crunching down louder than before. He wants to show Luom how satisfied he is with his food. The man is indeed a *Bac Giai*. His eyes stare out at his fish pond, and he says in a cold tone, "Take this rice and go home. Don't ever come back again. You do not need to pay it back."

Luom's dignity melts into the ground. She feels utterly humiliated, but knows that she will need this for tomorrow. Bowing, Luom responds politely, "Thank you, Mr. and Mrs. Tu. I'll never bother you again."

As Luom makes her way home, tears swiftly run down her cheeks. Angry at her lack of control, Luom grinds her teeth together. Mumbling in fierce tones to herself, she says, "Stupid girl! You seem to cry about everything! Go ahead and cry your heart out, but don't you dare let anyone see."

Back on the hammock at home, Mrs. Danh asks Luom, "Did you ask them for the rice?"

"Yes, Nanny."

Luom walks into her bedroom and quickly searches for some any dirty clothes. Piling them into her arms, she walks straight to the pond to wash them. Luom does not want her mother to see her tears. Vigorously scrubbing the clothes, she takes out all her anger on the cloth as she scolds herself.

"Luom, never again ask for anything from anyone. If you ever have any money, you must help your family. Find yourself a good husband. Make sure you search and search until you find a good man. Plunge your hand into the basket of the fish."

Unable to sleep that night, Luom thinks of the pictures of places in the books she has read. If she cannot explore outside of her daily routine, she understands she must plan her future through her books instead.

At 4:00 a.m. Luom looks at the can of rice and decides to cook just one-third. To ensure there is enough rice for everyone, she makes it very watery, which will give everyone a bowl of soup for the morning meal. Thank God, no one complains yet.

Luom and her siblings have their afternoon class, giving her time to prepare the midday meal as well. After breakfast, Luom says to her siblings, "We should go out to the rice field and play."

They are all excited to have a new adventure. Luom takes a small bamboo basket, a short knife and two sacks with her. As they walk along, Luom pulls up all the wild plants she recognizes and tosses them in the sack. Thu Huong digs snails out of the mud with the knife and these go in the sack, too. The siblings still think they are playing, and one asks, "Why are we picking these?"

Luom looks at all of them. "Do we like to play out here?" They respond enthusiastically, "Yes!"

"Then while we're playing, we pick our food, so we don't waste our time."

Luom goes about teaching her sister Thu Huong to use the bamboo basket as a tool to slowly scoop up the dead plants. Sometimes mineral fishes appear in the basket and a couple of times they catch a big snakehead fish. When it jumps out at them, they squeal with joy.

"How far are we going, Sister Two?" Thu Huong asks.

"How about we go as far as Duc's house? Maybe he can join us."

"That's far," two of the littler ones say.

"But we'll get a lot of food."

Finally, they reach their cousin's house. Duc and his siblings are happy to see their cousins. All begin to head back to Luom's house. Everyone knows that Luom can't swim and is afraid of leeches. They secretly conspire to play a prank on their older sister before heading home. Searching for a body of water, they find one where the leeches float on top. Jumping in, they exclaim, "Sister Two, come here! It's not too deep. Look, it's just up to our necks."

Unaware of their plan, Luom sees water only up to their necks, and concludes that the pond must be very shallow. She walks right into the water hole. Slipping on the mud where her feet barely reach, she tries to make her way back to the side.

When she sees the leeches, panic immediately sets in. Thrashing in the water, she tries to reach the side of the water hole. Muddy water splashes into her face and her open mouth. Coughing and gasping, she struggles to reach the firmer ground. As Luom frantically paddles away from the leeches, all the kids get out of the water, pointing their fingers and laughing. The two little boys stand on the side, holding their stomachs and bobbing up and down with mirth.

Duc reaches out a hand to help his cousin out of the water. Luom, still too scared of the leeches, forgets to punish anyone.

When they arrive home, Luom takes all the food from that day's walk and prepares a meal. It turns out to be quite good, and there was enough for an entire lunch and dinner.

Chapter 29
Labor for Love

Meanwhile, the laundry business is not doing well, mainly because Luom does not have the right equipment for it. She already lost the GI's business, and even though she puts more time into tutoring, it doesn't make her enough money to buy rice. Luom considers their financial situation again and thinks of another plan. Going to her mother again, Luom suggests, "Nanny, if we are able to borrow some money, let me take a three- month course for typing to be a secretary. You sign the paper and I will get a job at the base to work for the Americans. It will help us get out of this situation."

Mrs. Danh immediately shakes her head. "No! Your father would kill me. It would be a shame on our family for you to work for the Americans. And if you have more education, you'll leave me just like your father."

"Nanny, it's nothing to be ashamed of. We need food."

"What about Quoi?"

"What *about* Quoi, Nanny? He cannot help us."

"I mean, what would he say if I let you go work for the Americans?"

"Nanny, I don't care! I only care about us right now."

It seemed no matter what Luom's ideas are; Mrs. Danh will not grant her request.

"No, scrounge up what you can."

"Scrounge up what, Nanny? Look around you. We have nothing but this huge house."

"Why are you fighting with me, Luom?"

"Nanny, your children are starving. I could turn the situation around."

"What are you going to do? Marry an American?"

"That is a great idea. You thought about that, too?"

Mrs. Danh chuckles. "No, Luom, don't put words in my mouth."

"But you *have* thought about it. I'll do that."

"Luom, stop right there. You better go no further."

Luom stops arguing with her mother. The idea is now firmly planted in Luom's young mind, though Mrs. Danh only accidentally mentioned it.

The atmosphere is tense and suffocating, the path to her future a lightless tunnel. Luom struggles each day. Humming a cheerless song, she walks with the gloomy sky to keep her company. Suddenly, from the house Mrs. Danh screams out, "Luom!"

"Yes, I'm here, Nanny!" Luom, breathless, rushes back into the house.

"I'm about to have a baby."

The children chorus, "Nanny will have a baby!"

"Thu Huong," Luom orders, taking charge, "Stay home and take care of the children. I will take Nanny to the hospital."

"Yes."

Quickly, Luom rolls her bicycle out and crosses the bridge. Thu Huong helps Mrs. Danh to sit on the back and the pair rides off.

Luom pushes hard against the pedals, trying to reach the hospital as soon as possible. It is the same road she takes to school every day, but now Luom senses this journey will be tougher than ever before. Reflecting on her past experience, it was a good thing she used to carry her teacher home.

Every so often, the bike bounces against the rough surface of the road, bumping Mrs. Danh up and down. She groans and Luom can almost feel her mother's pain. She is concerned the baby might be born on the street before she reaches the hospital.

Mrs. Danh suffers from two pains simultaneously, one from her heart and the other from the baby. Luom cannot share either of these hurts. She loves her mother greatly despite her sometimes cruel words. Deep down, Luom understands her mother does not mean the things she says. Mrs. Danh always tells Luom, "You resemble your father."

Luom is strong enough to bring her pregnant mother to the hospital without incident. Quickly, Luom helps her mother into the emergency room. Nurses and doctors rush Mrs. Danh into the labor room.

A half-hour later, while Luom's mind overflows with worry, a nurse runs out to tell her the news. Mrs. Danh has delivered a baby boy, but he is premature and weighs only one kilo. Mrs. Danh and the baby are both in serious condition and short on nutrition. The doctor gives Mrs. Danh some medicine and puts the baby in special care.

Luom fearfully walks in to see her mother. Softly she asks, "Nanny, I'm here, how are you feeling?"

Mrs. Danh shakes her head and holds her daughter's hand as streams of tears pour down her face. Luom's tears fall beside her mother's. Mrs. Danh looks up to fix her eyes on her daughter. "I know how you take care of me and the children. You're a good person— without you, I don't know what I would do. Thank you."

Luom is taken by surprise at her mother's words. All the unpleasant memories suddenly vanish from Luom's mind and the hard feelings that she carried dissipate. Love replaces them. For a mother in this country to recognize and thank her daughter for her efforts is extremely rare. It is considered an unspoken responsibility for the oldest child in the family to act as a parent when the parents are not present, or if they can no longer function.

A memory flashes into Luom's mind of her first job, when she carried her brothers Diep and Tuan. Always balanced on her hips, with their arms wrapped around, her hip turned rough like the surface of the moon.

Mrs. Danh brings Luom out of her thoughts to ask, "Will you go see your brother for me?"

"Yes! I will, Nanny."

Luom feels a slight panic at leaving her mother in such a bad condition, but she has no other choice. She heads to the nursery to see her newborn baby brother. The baby lies in an incubator, not moving.

Every bone is etched out against his skin; he looks like a skeleton, barely alive.

The doctor told her there is only a twenty percent chance that he might live. Staring down at his small form, Luom can only feel sorrow. Suddenly, pain strikes her stomach, and dizziness overcomes her. She knows she must leave her brother before she faints. Quickly pulling her hair across her eyes, she hides her tears and leaves the room.

Her mother wanted to go against God's will, wanted to avoid having five sons in the family. Yet in the end a fifth son comes to her. Her mother loses the battle of love.

Luom knows her father will use this superstition as the final reason not to come home. It is clear he wants out, even as Mrs. Danh tries to hang onto the crumbling marriage.

Returning to her mother's room, Luom's mind is filled with depression. She wants to crawl into the corner of some room, any room, and rock herself to sleep. But she knows she must keep going. Aloud, Luom suggests to her mother, "Nanny, I'll write a letter to Ba Ngoai."

"I wonder if she's been released yet. How is your brother?"

"My brother is fine, Nanny, and she must be free by now. I'll come back tomorrow."

The sun had long gone down when Luom left her mother in the hospital. The streetlights cast eerie glows on the ground. Racing home as fast as she can on her bike, Luom knows her siblings must be hungry by now. As she approaches the house, she sees the children are waiting for her on the bridge as usual. They accost her with questions once she is in range of their voices.

"Where is our Nanny? Is she in the hospital? Is she having the baby yet?"

Luom responds in a calming tone, "Yes, Nanny is in the hospital and the baby is a boy."

Si asks in a small voice, "When are they coming home?"

"Maybe in a week."

Surprised shouts come from all the children "A week! That is a long time."

The children follow their older sister into the house. It is dark, and the emptiness seems to make them only feel worse. Thu Huong starts the oil lamp while Luom heads to the kitchen to cook. Thu Huong seems more quiet than usual. Diep and Tuan are also in deep thought. Dung and Si are too young to worry.

They eat supper without their mother that night, already missing her presence. Even though she usually lies motionlessly on the hammock for hours at a time, it is still comforting to know she is there for them. The Vietnamese always say, "A person without his mother is like a snake without its head, and a mother's love is vast and measureless, like the endless ocean." The children also love their father, but they understand that he no longer wants them, and they know they cannot force someone to love them.

The pot of rice holds just enough for all of them to eat a little bowl. On the side there are two boiled eggs to share for flavor. The food barely fills their stomachs. However, the children know that is all they have, so to fill themselves they toss down glasses of water from the pond.

Luom feels bitter, knowing she must send word of the baby to her father. "Thu Huong, tomorrow I want you to go to Ba Noi (Grandmother Ho Thiet) and let her know about Nanny's baby."

"Yes, I will."

Luom then turns to her brothers Diep and Tuan, "I want you two to stay home and watch Dung and Si. After I cook your breakfast, I will go to the bus station and send a letter to Ba Ngoai."

Diep asks, "What about our school?"

"We'll have to take a day off."

Thu Huong finds clothing for the boys, and Diep and Tuan take the two youngest to shower. Dung is wheezing because of his asthma. Mr. Bay is a heavy smoker. Mrs. Danh has been breathing in secondhand smoke for the past twenty-five years, and her lungs are damaged badly. There is no medication for either of them.

Si always sleeps with Mrs. Danh and tonight he misses her. Starting to cry, he asks for his mother. Luom walks over to comfort him, wrapping him in her arms to say quietly, "Si baby, tonight you sleep with Sister Thu Huong and I'll sleep with your brother Dung. He is sick. Tomorrow I'll take all of you to go see Nanny and our new baby brother."

Si is whimpering, but manages to smile at the news. "Tomorrow, we are going to see Nanny."

They are happy that they will all see their mother tomorrow. The children begin to chatter, voicing their hopes. "I want tonight to be a short night."

Like a drill sergeant, Luom orders, "It will be, but now all of you hop into bed."

Luom sets her brother Dung on her mother's bed and says, "You try to go to sleep, I'm writing a letter to Ba Ngoai at the table next to you. Don't you worry, I'm here for you."

Every time something happens, the night seems to lengthen. Dung's asthma is getting worse. The doctor always said there was nothing they could do for him. When there was money, Mrs. Danh would go to a Chinese herbalist and buy medicine for her son. The asthma never went away.

While Luom writes the letter to Grandmother Duong, she can hear Dung's breathing worsen. She ends the letter to Mrs. Duong quickly with a few words, "Ba Ngoai, Nanny had a baby." Then she folds the note in two and seals it. Luom rushes to her brother, sitting and holding him in her arms as he fights for breath and his life. The battle goes on for long hours before Dung relaxes his breathing back to normal.

"*Coo, coo, coo, coo.*"

The crowing from the neighborhood rooster tells Luom that it is four in the morning. She gets up, stepping into the kitchen to cook rice soup. Dung seems to be resting comfortably after his long night fighting asthma. Luom feels more at ease. Standing next to her sister's bed, Luom whispers, "Thu Huong, I have to go. Feed the kids before you go to Ba Noi."

She addresses her brothers next. "Diep and Tuan, make sure you guys watch the boys. Don't go near the pond."

Si, awakened by the conversation, worries that Luom will disappear like his mother. "Are you coming back home?" he asks.

Stroking her brother's back, Luom says to him. "I'll come back after I make a stop at the market. I have to cook food for Nanny, and I want all of you to stay in the house today and be good. We will visit Nanny before lunch."

Si claps his hands. Luom leaves the house and rides her bike to the bus station. It is the fastest way to send the letter, faster than the post office. The bus driver will stop at her grandmother's village and hand it to someone. Whoever gets the letter will deliver it Luom's uncle's house. Luom's cousins will give it to Mrs. Duong.

The bus station is always in chaos, and Luom uses her loud voice to get the attention of the bus driver. At last, she finds someone willing to take the letter. She offers to pay, but the bus driver assures her, "Someone on the bus will stop there anyway. I don't have to make a special stop, so don't worry about paying me."

Luom is happy that he is so nice; he could have charged her a fee.

Luom leaves the crowded bus station behind, and wasting no time, she bikes straight to the market and then home. Looking at her mother's wedding ring in the palm of her hand, she hesitates before walking into the pawnshop. This way she can have some money to pay for the food. Mrs. Danh never wore the ring anyway. Luom had been wearing it on her finger for a long time.

After leaving the pawnshop, Luom buys some pork and rice. By 8:00 am, she is already home and cooking. Thu Huong is also home. The family heads to the hospital soon after to see their mother. On the way, once in a while, they stop for Dung to catch his breath. The two youngest are unable to walk long distances, so the older siblings take turns giving their brothers piggy back rides.

When the children reach the hospital, Luom instructs everyone to keep quiet. They tiptoe into Mrs. Danh's room and their mother is happily surprised to see her children. The two youngest boys hop onto the bed to share her food. The pork that Luom cooked for Mrs. Danh is spicy and the boys stick their tongues out, scrunching up their faces. Mrs. Danh seems cheerful, but the children cannot stay too long.

The hospital has listed their family as poor, so they do not have to pay. Mrs. Danh is discharged after a week. The baby is still as tiny as when he was born, but Mrs. Danh is incapable of providing milk for her infant. Luom must use rice water instead to feed her little brother.

Word comes home from Major Bay, instructing the baby to be named Thanh Dien. Nothing is said about when he will be coming home.

Luom lets her sister and brothers go back to school the next day, but she remains home to care for her mother and three of the boys.

A few days later, while the children play outside in the afternoon sun, Luom hears them yelling, "Ba Ngoai! Ba Ngoai!"

She is hanging the laundry nearby and hastily throws the last piece of linen onto the line before running up to Grandmother Duong with the others. Dung and Si grab the bags from Mrs. Duong's hand and Luom is happy and grateful to her grandmother, as always. Grandmother Duong always appears like an angel and savoir; she is everything to Luom.

Mrs. Duong walks into the house to see her daughter and new grandson. Mrs. Danh's face is turned to the wall as always, while she holds her newborn son in her arms. Mrs. Duong calls out to her daughter, "Danh, this is Mother."

Mrs. Duong's presence allows Mrs. Danh to succumb to her feelings, enveloped in the power of her mother's love. She is no longer able to be a strong woman. The tears pour down her face. The sound of her weeping is extremely painful.

Mrs. Duong comforts her daughter in her arms, and they cry together. She feels sorry for making her daughter marry Major Bay. She wipes away the tears and gazes at the baby, saying, "I don't know how he's going to survive. He is so tiny."

She makes a noise with her tongue, inhaling slowly and exhaling with a mutter of worry. Luom answers her grandmother, "I don't know either."

Mrs. Duong plans to stay with her daughter and grandchildren for a while, allowing Luom to return to school tomorrow. Luom is happy, as she knows their life with Mrs. Duong will be more relaxing. She always listens to her grandmother. Though uneducated, Mrs. Duong is a wise person. Whatever she tries to teach her, right or wrong, Luom does whatever her grandmother suggests.

Chapter 30
Heartless

Two weeks have passed since Mrs. Danh came home from the hospital. Major Bay's youngest brother, Ut Mot, finally shows up for a brief and cold visit to Mrs. Danh. Before he leaves, Ut Mot takes a wallet and places it on the worship table. Luom wonders to whom it belongs. She opens it and learns that it is in fact her uncle's wallet. Inside, there is a picture of a little girl, the same one whom she saw at Ba Di Nam's house.

Luom is furious. She knows her uncle intended to put it there as a message, rather than tell her mother straight to her face. He couldn't have picked worse timing. Mrs. Danh has given birth and it amazes Luom how cruel people can be. Her father's family has no mercy for Mrs. Danh and the children.

A half hour later, Ut Mot returns. Luom waits for him at the front door. Before handing over the wallet, she opens it to the picture, asking him, "Uncle, is this *your* wallet?"

He yanks it out of Luom's hand. "Yes!"

Glaring at her uncle, she asks, "Uncle, why would you put this on the table? Isn't it supposed to stay in your pocket? You want to show us something?"

Not caring that her uncle is fuming, Luom continues on. She points her finger to the little girl's picture. "Who is this little girl?"

Surprised at Luom's disrespectful words and direct manner, Ut

Mot quickly becomes angrier. He answers her in dark tones, "*This* is my niece."

"And why don't I know this already?"

Ut Mot's eyes are in flaming. He is incapable of carrying on a fight with his niece with words. Major Bay's family has shown Luom their wicked ways and she cannot ignore it. It is outrageous for them to treat Mrs. Danh like this. They cripple her soul. Especially when Mrs. Danh is still sick and weak from childbirth.

Ut Mot answers Luom's last question. "This is my wife's side of the family."

Luom is annoyed even more by her uncle's answer. He is lying. Even he knows that she knows he is lying. She counters, "I know all the people in your family." Luom pushes her uncle into the corner

He threatens her, saying, "I'll tell Ba Noi, and she will come here and kill you."

Luom fixes her eyes on her uncle's face. "Go on then, I'm not afraid of you people anymore."

Ut Mot is quickly out the door. One hour later, her other grandmother, Mrs. Ho Thiet, bursts into Luom's house. Mrs. Thiet does not bother to say hello to Mrs. Duong. She sits at the front of the bed until Luom comes over, crosses her arms, and bows. "Hello, Ba Noi."

Pointing an accusing finger at Luom, Mrs. Ho Thiet begins to scream. "You're a disgrace to me, to your father, your mother, your uncle and both sides of the family!"

"Ba Noi you mean I'm a disappointment to you and *your* family. There is no complaint from Ba Ngoai's side of the family."

Luom's remark causes great displeasure and humiliation for Mrs. Ho Thiet. She suddenly throws a temper tantrum. Making a fist with both hands, she beats her chest like a drum, screaming for God to strike Luom with lighting.

Luom knows she is supposed to calm her grandmother with false sweet talk and ask for forgiveness, but she does nothing of the kind. Mrs. Ho Thiet realizes she cannot move her granddaughter to tears this way. It is a characteristic Luom inherited from her father and Mrs. Ho Thiet herself. Now she can take some of her own medicine.

Realizing this, Mrs. Ho Thiet changes tactics. She calms herself, and pulls out her tobacco and chewing stuff to mash in a tiny cup. Pouring it into her mouth, she chews slowly and then continues the assault on Luom. "Why do you question your uncle? In this family, there are no other children like you. From this day forward, I want you to obey and shut your shrewish mouth."

Unfortunately, Luom is on the path to completely losing control and can hardly think to consider what will happen to her when her father finds out. She also knows it is her only chance to make a point. "Ba Noi, Uncle is not an honest person. He could just tell the truth or say nothing at all. You all think I'm stupid."

Mrs. Ho Thiet is even angrier, "Well, why don't you sit on your uncle's face then?"

Luom laughs aloud at her grandmother. "Uncle is just like father to you. Why are you telling me to do the disrespectful thing?"

Mrs. Duong smacks the back of Luom's head and says through her teeth, "Shut your mouth, little girl. You've said enough. Your life is on a string."

This has no effect on Luom. She is determined that her father and all of his family feel sorry for abandoning his first family for the rest of their lives. After all, Luom will be carrying this burden for the rest of hers. If they ever feel remorse and ask for forgiveness, Luom will never forgive them.

She turns to face Mrs. Ho Thiet once again. "Ba Noi, why are you angry with me? You know, you should ask yourself, whose fault is it?"

Mrs. Ho Thiet runs to Mrs. Danh's hammock, but she shouts at Luom over her shoulder. "I'll tell your father! He'll use the horse to pull you into pieces or bury you alive. He'll bury you standing with your head above ground and use the buffalos to walk on top of you! You are a bastard!"

Luom adds to the heat of her grandmother's rage. "Yes!" she exclaims. "I was a bastard a long time ago, don't you know? I and all of the children are in this house are bastards."

Mrs. Ho Thiet looks fiercely at Luom and then runs out of the house. Instantly, Mrs. Danh gets off her hammock. She does not bother to ask Luom what has just happened, for it is clear she already knows. Pointing her finger at her daughter's face, she says, "I want you to get out of my house right now. You just broke up my family's happiness."

Luom stands rooted to the spot, looking at her mother in shock. She cannot believe the words that just came from her mother's lips. Luom is the only person defending her while everyone else shrinks in fear of her father. If Luom had had the chance to think, she would fear for her life.

Luom is shocked, but she also knows her mother is worried about what will happen to her when Major Bay comes home. Still, Luom has to say, "What happiness? You love him so much, you're blind."

Mrs. Danh only says in her anger, "Bastard, bastard."

The situation is out of control. It takes Mrs. Duong to pull Luom away as she pushes Mrs. Danh back to her hammock. "Danh, you should think before you open your mouth."

Luom is hurt deeply by her mother's words. Having no more word to say to Mrs. Danh, she walks to the pond and scoops up water for the laundry. Mrs. Duong comes out and sits next to Luom. "Try to understand your Nanny, she's not as bad as she seems."

Scrubbing the clothes vigorously, Luom answers, "I'm trying, Ba Ngoai, but I'm still a child."

Mrs. Duong loves her granddaughter very much, but does not want any bloodshed between the two families. If something happens, Bay Thoi, Mrs. Duong's son, would be the one to start it. Her son had to make a deal to become a secret agent for the Viet Cong in order for Mrs. Duong to be released. He now lives a double life. Luom has suspected that for a long time. In fact, she had even used it as an excuse for her father leaving the family.

The war in this country had created too many problems for too many families, all because of the actions of older generations. Luom loves both of her parents, but her father's abandonment of his family has made things so bad that something should be done. She understands her mother's feelings. And yet, Luom's heart is wounded by her mother.

Mrs. Duong is aware that eventually her granddaughter will crack, and she is worried for Luom when her son-in-law returns home. She tells Luom, "For you to remain here, it's a helpless situation. If you stay here, they will make you marry someone you do not love. I want you to break away, break from our customs. Go do something for your life. I feel sorry that I pushed your nanny into this family. Your father is a good person, but his mother will always dominate him. They found too many ways to keep him entangled. I'm glad I have all of you. You are all wonderful grandchildren. I love all of you, especially you, Luom. I don't care what the gossip will be. Just go do something for yourself, no matter what it might be. Always love your Nanny and your siblings. And remember, they don't have your brains."

Mrs. Duong hands Luom some money. "Take your mother's wedding ring out of the pawn shop before heaven falls and the earth crumbles."

Luom's tears roll down her face. Mrs. Duong walks inside to let Mrs. Danh know that she will be going home tomorrow. Mrs. Duong is always lending a hand to Luom. This time Mrs. Duong has to imagine what would happen to Luom if she stays. Worst of all, Mrs. Duong suspects that Bay Thoi wants to use Luom to get her father. He sends notes to Major Bay threatening, "I'll tell Luom to come down and deal with you."

The truth is that Mr. Bay and Mrs. Danh both love their children very much, but the war is turning their lives in a different direction. Mrs. Duong is right. It's not that Luom's father is bad; it's just that his life got a bad start. He must be a good son to his mother, for that is the Chinese way, even if it means leaving his first wife and children. However, that is only one of the reasons Major Bay had to leave his family. He planned his journey well. He could not plan only for himself his wife and their children. No matter how old he is, Major Bay has to please his mother.

For a grandmother to tell her granddaughter to run away is unheard of in Vietnam. The future is uncertain and Mrs. Duong is unable to foresee what will happen to Luom. However, she has faith in her granddaughter's knowledge and education. To her, Luom is the smartest one in the family.

What she does not know is that Luom so far knows nothing. Really, it is just the beginning and she has far more to learn.

Chapter 31
Waiting for Verdict

While Luom waits for Major Bay to come home, she thinks about how to face her father. She reminds herself of the old Vietnamese saying, "*Hum du, cung khong the an thit con.*" (Even the lions do not eat their younger.) Her father is not a terrible man. And yet, Luom will never forget the time he pointed a gun at her mother's head. The image keeps flashing again and again in her mind.

The parents of one of Luom's friends live in Sai Gon and Luom can stay with the family for a while. She plans to finish high school later, somehow.

Before leaving, Luom decides to tell Quoi goodbye and make sure there are no regrets.

She finds Quoi's address that had been hidden inside her book and rides her bike to see him. At her age to visit a man is forbidden and if people find out, a bad reputation could follow her for a long time. However, she must make the trip. When she arrives, she can already feel the neighbors' eyes on her, and can almost hear the quiet hissing of their lips. She takes Quoi and leads him out to the rice field.

Both sit together at the edge of the canal, watching the water flow. Quoi talks quietly, planning for their future, but all Luom can think about are the days ahead. She wonders if she should tell Quoi about her family problems. Perhaps he will have some idea of how to help her.

After hearing her explain the situation, Quoi only says to her, "Your family is rich and your father has high rank in the military. You have nothing to complain about."

It is shocking at first to hear those words from the man who wants to be her husband. Then suddenly, Luom realizes in that moment that she and Quoi are nothing alike. He could have shown some hint of concern, or he could have kept silent, but he said what he said. The feeling of guilt at the thought of ending their relationship washes away. She returns to her original purpose: to tell him goodbye.

As her uneasiness returns, she is speechless. Her eyes stare at the endless water flow of the canal. Quoi's voice is now a dull echo against her ears. Unable to continue sitting beside Quoi any longer, Luom says abruptly, "I have to go home."

He turns to her. "Why so sudden? My brother will come in a few days to check on you."

"Why would he want to do that?"

"Because I wanting to marry you. I have to ask for his approval along with the rest of the family."

"You mean you have to ask their permission?"

"Of course, didn't you know that?"

"No, I didn't know that, I thought you loved me and that was it."

"No. It's just like with you, I have to get consent from your parents, too."

"That's different."

"Silly, how is it different?"

"Be a man. You have to think on your own. What happens if your brother says no?"

"I know my brother. He'll say yes."

"And what if he says no?"

"I love you, everyone will love you."

"You mean I will live my life with your family to judge me? I have to go."

Luom picks up her bike and rides off, leaving Quoi behind.

On the way home, emptiness fills her as a buzzing clouds her mind. But it's easy for her to walk away, thank God. Luom realized just in time that Quoi is not the man for her. There are plenty of fish in the sea. Luom is thankful that her parents brought her into this life and she understands how much her parents have taken care of her. She renews her resolve to return the favor by marrying someone she loves. Quoi is so uncaring about her family; he does not deserve to marry her. And with a husband like Quoi , Luom fears she will face his family by herself, like Mr. Ngoc's first wife did.

Luom remembers the story Mrs. Danh told her, about Mrs. Ho Thiet forcing one of her daughter in-laws to carry a pot of burned fishes on top of her head, walking three miles to show her parents that she ruined her husband's supper. Luom could not see herself living that life.

When Luom reaches home, she sees Mrs. Danh has been waiting for her at the front door. As soon as she spots Luom, she yells, "Where were you all day?"

Luom sets her bike against the corner of the house and says without looking up, "I have things to do, Nanny."

"What are these things that you have to do besides caring for your siblings and me?"

Now looking at the unhappy face of her mother, Luom just wants to walk away in silence, but out of respect, she forces herself to answer. "I had to seek a friend."

"What friend?"

"Just a friend."

For some reason, Mrs. Danh lets it go. Luom continues into the house and gathers the dirty clothes to wash.

Unsure of when she should leave, Luom's schoolwork is slipping. The thought of it is no longer in her mind. She is struggling. Sometimes while tutoring the kids, she finds herself staring at empty space. It has become extremely difficult to put food on the table. Luom remembers that Mrs. Duong mentioned before, that she exhausted the finances to help her, and was uncertain how long she could continue.

If Luom chooses to stay, then she would carry on the tradition of reliance on someone else to support her. She doesn't want to see herself marrying someone like her father. And it is not her grandparents' and her uncles' responsibility to support her.

Somehow, Luom will have to save a little money to make the trip. One question is always on her mind, though: what is she going to do in the big city?

Luom remembers reading about some girls who went to Sai Gon. In the beginning, they had to be maids for someone, but later they found something better. Luom thinks she might be able to do just that. A friend had already set up a housecleaning job in the city for her. Two days later, Quoi and his brother come to visit Mrs. Danh. Quoi's brother has already consented for him to marry Luom. Luom doesn't care. Quoi is no longer on her mind. She has many dreams for her future, but marrying Quoi and becoming a teacher is out of the question. She wants other futures: to become a *Cai Luong* actress,(similar to an opera singer,) or marry an American. All she knows is that she wants to live a comfortable life, and not struggle like her mother.

Chapter 32
Into the Unknown

The time has come for Luom to leave. She has enough money saved for her trip. Before taking off, Luom ensures that the laundry is washed and food is in the house. At 4:00 in the morning, Luom cooks the rice soup, puts some rice water in a baby bottle for her little brother and places her mother's wedding ring on her grandfather's worshipping table. Luom had been saving the ring for a while since Mrs. Danh had not wanted to wear her wedding band for a long time. She writes a short note and leaves the house quickly.

On the bridge, a group of neighborhood police officers stand guard. One of the cops, seeing her approaching form, shouts out to her. "Who are you?"

Luom answers, "My name is Luom."

As soon as she says her name, everyone recognizes her; most people around the neighborhood know how hard she works for her family. Another cop says, "Go home, come back at 6:00 am and we'll let you through."

For the first time in her life, Luom is afraid of getting shot. She wastes no time, rushing back into the house she had just left so quickly. She slides the wedding ring once again onto her finger and tears up the note. Taking a deep breath, she continues with her daily routine while the house sleeps. It is summer and school is out, so everyone rests until late in the morning.

When they awake, no one notices that she ever left.

The next morning, Luom waits until 5:30 am to begin her journey. By the time she arrives at the bridge, all the police officers are gone and the bridge is busy as usual. Luom walks to the bus station, pays the bus driver, and hops on the bus.

The tires of the bus roll up and down, over and over on the road and her stomach rolls with them. A new chapter of her life is about to begin, a life without all the people that she loves. There is no turning back now.

Luom is uncertain of the outcome. Normally, she would enjoy the beautiful landscape of her country, but in this moment, there are millions of ants crawling in her stomach. She asks herself, "Where is my future headed?'

As people board and leave the bus, casual conversation and laughter mingle together. Again, she asks herself, "How can I abandon my family so easily?"

Luom reassures herself. "I'm not abandoning all of you, I'm just going to find work and I'll send for you later." Memories of her mother's face and of her siblings' faces make a strong presence in her mind, but her father's image has already blurred.

Luom wonders, "How can I forget about my father so quickly?" He had been a good father and good husband to her mother before. What went wrong with her family? For many years they had remained together through the twists and turns of life, and then, so suddenly, the family went to pieces. It was all because of one woman, a woman Mrs. Danh had trusted, accepted into the family, and treated as her own sister. Mrs. Danh had no idea that with her acceptance, she also gave her husband consent to be with another woman. Mrs. Danh's mind is pure and trusting. Unlike Luom, Mrs. Danh was never suspicious of anyone.

Many more thoughts race through her mind before the bus reaches Sai Gon. Luom rides a xich lo dap to her friend's mother's house. That night, the first thing she does is to help the family prepare the evening meal. After they eat, they order Luom to wash the dishes and put their little girl to bed.

Luom soaks the clothes in the bucket and washes them after the girl falls asleep. She will be sleeping with Luom from now on. At only a year old, she is adorable and Luom immediately bonds with her.

Luom sits outside of the house, washing their laundry. Her tears drop in quick succession as she listens to everyone enjoying the evening inside the house's warm glow.

Luom looks up at the sky and asks herself, "What did you get yourself into? This woman has nine kids. That's more than your mother has. You cannot be her maid and help your mother on a salary of one dollar a month."

The stars in the night sky are not clustered like at home. The sky at home gave Luom words for her songs. She would go outside, spin around and count its stars. Here, the sky gives her only tears. Silently, she promises herself, "Luom, you will do better."

Epilogue

While Luom was deep in thought, a familiar, sweet voice took her suddenly back to the present. Twisting her chin up, Luom saw her husband, Chris, standing behind her.

"What are you doing, Honey?" he asked.

"Oh, I just went back to my past."

"How far did you get?"

Luom reached up to take the cup of coffee Chris held out to her. "Oh, just halfway."

"Perhaps another time you'll make it all the way through."

"Yes, it's possible."

"The kids are still sleeping?"

"Yes, sound asleep."

Luom and Chris cuddled next to each other at the kitchen table, sipping their coffee and admiring their view of the countryside as the rain fell gently. The landscaped palm trees danced in the wind and the thunder rumbled in the distance, getting further away.

Leaning on her husband's shoulder, Luom felt the strength of his love. Luom searched for him for many years, for a man devoted to family, though she may not have known it. Luom kept faith in God, who blessed her and sent angels to look after her, all those years. To Luom, everyone she met through her whole life were all her angels. The bad things that happened to her, Luom believes, were from angels of darkness, showing her whom to avoid. Luom learned from the good things people did for her, and always reminded herself to be appreciative. To be a wife, mother, and grandmother, with all the angels around her, filled her with a boundless pride, as measureless as the ocean.

Even after all this time, tried by the hardships of life, Luom remembered her two most important angels: her parents. If they had not done what they did, Luom would never have come so far. Her parents gave all their knowledge to their children, and to Luom especially: how to be brave, how to sacrifice for those you love, how to comfort them, how to keep them safe.

If she could start her life over, Luom thought, she would not change it at all. She would keep all of the people in her life, even the bad ones. They made her life hers, a single life, unique, defined by her grandparents, Major Bay, Mrs. Danh, and most importantly, herself.

Sometimes Luom will wonder: is this the journey she chose, or has her journey been set by God? The war made a bridge, brought her to America for a better life, and God brought her to the man of her dreams. Still, how much came from Luom, and how much was from the angels?

But these are impossible questions, which only faith can truly answer. Strongly Luom believed as she whispered, "Thank you, God. Nanny, thank you. Father, and everyone who passed through my life who helped me, thank you. I love you all."

TheEnd

About the Author

My Fenton was born and raised in southern Vietnam. My Fenton came to the United State forty-one years ago. She now lives with her husband and with her two sons in San Diego, California.

In 2005 she reunited with her sister, Thu Huong. Thu Huong and Thu Huong's family now settle near Little Saigon in Westminster, California.

My is friends with several members of the Vietnamese-American literary movement in San Diego, California, such as Mr. Le Bao Ky, the author, Mrs. Ho Huong Loc, the poet, and Mr. Nguyen Hong, the composer.

Although this is her first book, Mrs. Fenton has a wealth of other material, due to the fact that she will type whatever comes to mind. When My is away from the keyboard, she spends her time sewing, constructing flower arrangements, singing, and cooking.

As a retired seamstress, My now devotes her attention and affection to her husband, her children, and is a self-proclaimed very happy grandmother.

CPSIA information can be obtained at www.ICGtesting.com
Printed in the USA
LVOW08s0546070813

346605LV00002B/6/P